MOUNTAIN BIKING IN WEST WALES

Dave & Barbara Palmer

Published by Sigma Leisure – an imprint of
Sigma Press, 1 South Oak Lane, Wilmslow, Cheshire SK9 6AR, England.

British Library Cataloguing in Publication Data
A CIP record for this book is available from the British Library.

ISBN: 1-85058-585-7

Typesetting and Design by: Sigma Press, Wilmslow, Cheshire.

Cover photograph: Barbara in Brechfa Forest (Ride 18)

Maps and photographs: The authors

Illustrations: Graham Skett

Printed by: MFP Design and Print

Disclaimer: the information in this book is given in good faith and is believed to be correct at the time of publication. No responsibility is accepted by either the author or publisher for errors or omissions, or for any loss or injury howsoever caused. Only you can judge your own fitness, competence and experience.

Preface

This book is intended both for the tourist to the area and for local people who would like to find suitable and interesting places to take their Mountain bikes.

We have noticed that every year many people visit the area and bring their bikes, but very few actually ride them. Our research has shown that this is because they simply do not know where to go. This guide therefore aims to direct the cyclist to the best and most interesting routes to ride in the area.

Consideration has been given to using very quiet roads and tracks wherever possible. All of these rides have been ridden by mature adults of both sexes and also by young boys. On some of these rides we have been able to take a toddler in a seat attached to the back. We have indicated the suitability for this at the start of the ride.

The rides can be as difficult or as easy as you wish to make them. If you want a challenge then you can ride everywhere, and ride quickly. If this is still not challenging enough then you may like to combine two rides together. The majority of people though, we expect, will be quite happy to do the rides at the pace we did; ambling along and stopping to enjoy the views, with maybe a picnic or a stop for a drink.

Please be very considerate of the fragile nature of the environment and do not ride your bike where it is likely to cause damage to wild life or destroy the ecology. This is a very beautiful area and must be kept so for future generations to enjoy.

Dave & Barbara Palmer

Acknowledgements

We would like to express our gratitude to the following people:

John, Jill, Ben & Tom Harrison, Sheila & Georgina Ravenscroft, Marie & Johnnie Davies, Tina & Neil, Karen & Anth who all rode along with us and helped to check the directions.

Our grandson David who bravely tested the baby seat.

Graham Skett for his wonderful sketches which he has allowed us to include.

Garry at Bierspool Cycles for keeping our bikes on the road.

Alan Shepherd for the kind use of his aerial photographs in the preparation of our maps.

The staff at Haverfordwest Tourist Information Centre.

Rob Donaldson & Roger Gates of Forest Enterprise, Llandovery.

Contents

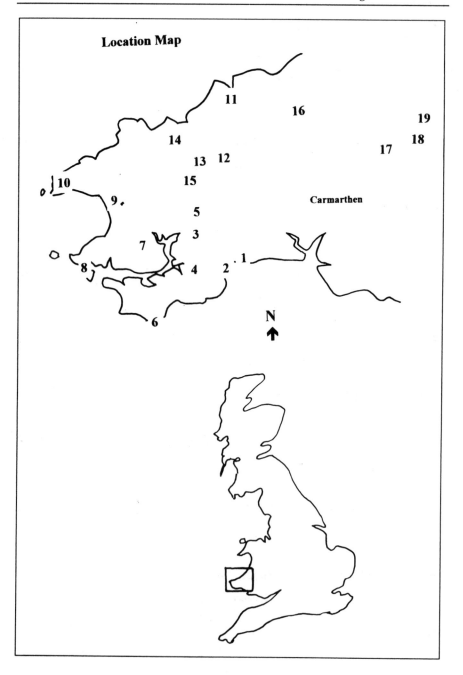

Location Map

West Wales: An Overview

The area known as West Wales includes Pembrokeshire, parts of Carmarthenshire and a section of Cardiganshire. The rides we have included in this book extend east as far as the Brechfa Forest, to the north as far as Cardigan, west to St David's Peninsula and in the south to Amroth and the start of the Pembrokeshire long distance coastal path.

It is an area of great contrasts. North Pembrokeshire is very quiet, rugged and wild, with the mystical Preseli hills presiding over it; South Pembrokeshire has more tourists, and a more serene, yet extremely beautiful countryside.

North and South Pembrokeshire are divided by an imaginary line known as the Landsker line, which roughly follows the main A40 road. This line represents the linguistic division between Welsh speakers in the north and "little England beyond Wales", an area where the English language predominates because of the settlement of the Norman's during the eleventh century.

Many castles were built south of the Landsker line by the Normans to control the Welsh, and to safeguard the Irish trade from Bristol, via the ports of Milford Haven and Tenby. Fine examples of these castles are Pembroke, Carew, Llawhaden, Tenby and Manorbier.

King Henry I also introduced an influx of Flemish settlers into South Pembrokeshire. They were very hard working and soon became very prosperous, and took over many Manor Houses and Castles. They were politically allied with the Normans and soon the Welsh were driven out into the poor farmland of the north. To this day a grudging animosity still exists between the north and the south.

The people of Carmarthenshire are very different from the people of Pembrokeshire. Carmarthenshire is predominately Welsh speaking – some older people do not speak English, so it simply is not true that locals only start speaking Welsh in the presence of tourists.

After all – you expect French to be spoken in France! Welsh people love to have a chat and will only be too happy to tell you all the tales and folklore of the area.

In the west and south-west the climate is very mild due to the warming influence of the Gulf Stream and it is very unusual to have snow. If you travel eastwards to St Clears or north past Cardigan, the climate is much colder and snow is commonplace in the winter.

The warmest and driest months are May, June and July and are ideal for biking. August is warm but you may have the odd wet day. Although colder, September and October can be pleasant with not much rain. The worst months are November and December, known locally as the monsoon period. Usually from Bonfire night until Christmas it rains persistently. If you don't mind the cold in January, February, March and April, there are many pleasant days when you can go biking. You must be prepared to get muddy, however!

The prevailing winds are westerly and because of this there are not many trees on the extreme north-west coast. Any trees that are there have a distinct easterly tilt. It does however have an extremely beautiful rugged coastline. South-east Pembrokeshire, which faces across to Devon, is far softer, greener and has many trees. It is protected from the westerly winds by the Preseli hills. Some of the best beaches can be found here, for example Saundersfoot, Tenby, Broadhaven and Barafundel Bay.

The area is extremely abundant in flora and fauna. During the spring and summer the hedges are ablaze with wild flowers. Look out for the buzzard sitting on the power wires or hovering on the thermals. You will hear him plaintively meowing like a cat. The abundance of wildlife is far too extensive to describe here, but if you are interested, there are many books available on the subject.

Your Bike

Most of these rides involve a certain amount of off-road riding. Some tracks used can be extremely bumpy, sometimes boggy, muddy and overgrown, but this can be great fun if you have a sense of adventure.

We do not therefore recommend using an ordinary road or touring bike unless you are prepared for it to be damaged.

If you are purchasing a bike be sure that you buy the right size. The frame of a mountain bike has to be much smaller than that of a tourer, as you need to be able to get off and on easily. If you have to jump off it quickly and there is no clearance between your crotch and the cross-bar this could prove to be very painful! As a rough guide, there should be two to three inches of space between your crotch and the cross-bar of the bike when standing astride it.

A good all-terrain (mountain) bike is recommended. Expect to pay upwards of at least £200 for anything that will be durable. Cheaper bikes may cope with the roughness of the track but do not expect the brakes to be as efficient, so take extra care on steep descents.

You will often find yourself riding through water and mud and for this reason sealed bearings, only found in good quality mountain bikes, are preferable. If you use a cheaper bike then be prepared to have it serviced more often.

Sometimes, you do get punctures!

Hiring a bike

There are several places in the West Wales area where you may hire a bike. A list of places is included in the Appendix, but please telephone before starting out to ensure that bikes are still available.

Tools

Before starting out, ensure that you have a basic tool kit with you. Remember you will be out in the country and a long way from a garage or repair shop.

A basic tool kit should consist of an adjustable spanner, 4mm, 5mm and 6mm Allen keys, and a small Philips head screwdriver. You will also need a pump (make sure it is the right fitting for your tube), a puncture outfit and a set of tyre levers. We always carry a spare tube with us, as it is usually easier to fit a new tube and mend the punctured one when we get home.

What to Wear

If you are new to mountain biking, improvise with whatever clothing you have to hand. Jeans however are definitely not recommended. They are very uncomfortable to wear on a bike and if you should get wet they will make you extremely cold.

Make sure that you are wearing several layers of clothing that you can take on or off according to the weather conditions and your body temperature. You can get very hot when climbing hills and intensely cold when coming down a long descent.

In recent years wind proof jackets have become available. These look like a lightweight nylon kagoul, but they are made of a special material, usually Pertex, which keeps the wind out and is also shower-resistant. There are versions which are waterproof. We have found these to be excellent, as they are very light to carry and very pleasant to wear.

Lightweight wind proof fleeces are much better than jumpers when the weather is cold, as one fleece is worth several jumpers and much lighter to carry! In winter we usually wear a long-sleeved thermal vest, padded cycle shorts and thermal long johns as our base layer. We then add leggings, fleeces and wind proof as required. Hopefully in the summer you can leave the thermals off.

We prefer to wear waterproof hiking boots or shoes, as sometimes it is necessary to walk or wade across the mud, and it isn't pleasant to ride the next 20 miles with wet squelchy feet.

Maps

A good map is essential, preferably one with a scale of 1:25,000, though 1:50,000 will do, but from personal experience we find the larger scale better if for any reason we have to revise our journey. Most of the tourist information centres and good book shops in the area keep a stock of these and will advise you which is the appropriate one.

Compass

It is also advisable to take a compass. Some of these rides, particularly the ones in the Preseli hills and the Brechfa Forest can be scary if the mist comes down. Check your map regularly so that you always know where you are, and, if the weather does get bad you can easily find your way back by taking bearings. If you don't know how to use a compass, I suggest you get some instruction first!

First Aid Kit

Don't forget to pack a basic first aid kit. Useful items to take would be plasters, antiseptic cream and a crepe bandage. We have also found foil wrapped sachets of antiseptic wipes to be invaluable.

Food & Drink

Biking, particularly on difficult hilly terrain expends a lot of energy, and it is essential to have a supply of high energy food. Always pack a bigger picnic than you think you will need. It's better to have too much than to find you are starving and miles from anywhere. Nuts and raisins make very useful emergency provisions and are very easy to carry.

Emergency Money

Always carry some money. There aren't many shops or pubs on

these routes, but if you do find one it can be a bit of a downer if you haven't got enough to buy that lovely refreshing drink.

Caring for your Bike

Check your bike over before leaving and make sure that tyres are correctly inflated, and that brakes and gears are functioning correctly. If there is a lot of rough track riding, it is better to put less air in your tyres than you would when riding on the road. The range of tyre pressures is usually marked on the side of the tyres and the lower pressure would be more suitable off-road.

After returning from the ride make sure that you have enough energy to wash your bike down as it will probably be very muddy! Spray the cables, etc. with WD40 to drive out the water, and then oil with a good lube. Be careful not to get any lubricant on the wheel rims or brakes.

Know the route

The evening before the ride we suggest that you read through the route instructions and description of the ride, and check the instructions off against the map. This way it will be much easier when you are cycling. At the end of the ride we have included brief details of places of interest along the way.

Take Care

Remember mountain biking can be dangerous. Be careful and ride within your limitations and skill. There is no shame in getting off and walking. The idea is to enjoy yourself and not to impress others.

If you are going on one of the more remote rides, get a weather forecast before leaving. It can be very unnerving if the mist comes down and you are not prepared. Ride with a friend or at least let someone know where you are going. On one ride, Dave fell into a pit and was unable to get out unaided. This was very amusing at the time but would not have been so funny if he was alone and no one knew where he was.

Time Taken

The time that we quote is only given as a guide. If you are super-fit, you probably can do it in half the time, but do remember that you are also governed by the harshness of the terrain. Our average speeds ranged from 4mph to 8mph. This allowed for map reading, frequent stops to eat and drink, and time taken stopping to admire the scenery. If you're not used to cycling regularly over rough terrain, allow longer.

Legality of routes

We have taken care to try to ensure that the rides in the book can legally be used by cyclists, but we cannot be held responsible if you have any problems. It is not always possible to be absolutely certain of the legality of some rights of way. Please use your judgement and walk if in doubt.

Code of the Trail

- ¤ Only ride where it is legal and you will cause no damage. Dismount and walk if you are not sure.

- ¤ Be courteous, and give way to pedestrians and horses. Bicycles do not make much noise and if you come up behind people they may easily be startled and may walk into your path. This can be disastrous for all.

- ¤ Do not leave litter. Tidy up after yourself.

- ¤ Use gates and stiles to cross fences if possible. Be sure to close gates after you.

- ¤ Be considerate when crossing farm land. Do not damage crops or frighten animals.

- ¤ Don't light fires.

- ¤ If riding through Forestry Commission land, be extremely careful if logging is in operation. From time to time, some tracks may be closed. Please take notice of the signs and take an alternative route.

Mountain Biking can be a dangerous sport and the authors cannot be held responsible for any injuries or consequential losses which may be incurred while following any of these routes.

Ride 1: Amroth, Llanteg, Tavernspite, Amroth

Abbreviations: O.R.S. Off-road Section; R.S. Road Section.

Distance: 16 miles.

Time: 2 hours.

Terrain: Country lanes and bridleways. Two hard climbs, otherwise easy. This ride would be suitable to take a baby in a rear seat.

Map: Ordnance Survey Outdoor Leisure No 36, South Pembrokeshire.

Start and Finish: At Amroth car park. Grid Reference 164 070.

---

1.   Turn RIGHT out of the car park, go over the river bridge and at the T-junction with the sea facing you, turn LEFT.

2.   With the sea on your right proceed along the coast road passing a road on your left, then just past Amroth Castle Caravan Site turn LEFT on to a metalled footpath. Go between two cottages and soon the track starts to climb uphill towards Factory Wood.

3.   (O.R.S.) Ignore the track to your right. The track becomes gravelled and very steep. Keep on until you reach the metalled road at the top of the hill. On your right is a track to Trelessy Farm; continue STRAIGHT on along the road until you come to a T-junction in Llanteglos village.

4.   (R.S.) At the T-junction turn RIGHT and pass The Hunting Lodge Country Inn within 200m on your right.

5.   At a cross-roads with a pond on your left, go STRAIGHT on until you reach the main A477 trunk road at Llanteg.

6.   Go STRAIGHT on over the trunk road but take care this can be a busy road. If you would like a detour you could turn right and then left to visit Crunwere Old Church on the hill and then come back to the main road to carry on with your journey. Follow the

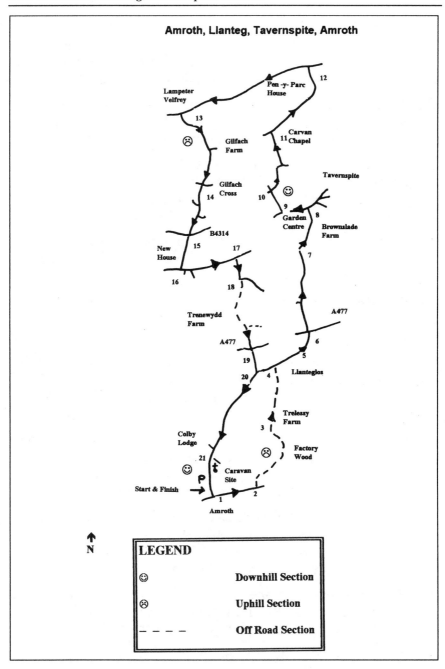

Amroth, Llanteg, Tavernspite, Amroth

sign to Tavernspite, pass the telephone box and start to climb up the hill. At the top of the hill ignore the road to your left and pass the house on your right called Highfield House. After passing Crunwere House on your left, the road starts to descend.

7. At about 4 miles into the journey you will pass under some power pylons. Soon after you will pass Brown Slade Farm on your right. Carry on to the five-way road junction in Tavernspite.

8. Go over the junction and turn LEFT by the village pump and follow the sign to Narberth. Pass the Alpha Inn on your left and very soon you will be at Tavernspite Garden Centre on your left, where they sell welcome cups of tea and cakes.

9. Pass the garden centre and carry on for about 100m until you reach the cross-roads and then turn RIGHT; signposted to Coarse Fishing.

10. Go down the hill and fork RIGHT. Pass the turning to Upper Carvan Farm on your right and carry on to the T-junction by Carvan Chapel which was built in 1797.

11. At the T-junction turn RIGHT ride along the road following the signs to Coarse Fishing and before long you will pass the large pond on your right where the fishing takes place. Climb uphill to a T-junction.

12. At the T-junction turn LEFT passing Pen-y-Park House and follow the sign post to Narberth. Ignore lanes to your right and left. Pass Bible Garden on your right and cross over an old stone river bridge and enter the outskirts of Lampeter Velfrey.

13. Turn LEFT up the hill and pass Greenfield Cottage on your right; this hill is quite a steep climb. At the top of the hill ignore the lane to the left to Gilfach Farm, approximately 10 miles into your journey, and carry on to the cross-roads at Gilfach Cross.

14. Go STRAIGHT on at the cross-roads. Ignore the road to your right and pass Penfford House on your left. Ignore the lane to your left and then go down the hill to the cross-roads.

15. At the cross-roads over the B4314 go STRAIGHT on. Soon you will pass New House on your right which is the source of Princess Gate Spring Water.

16. When you reach the staggered cross-roads turn LEFT towards Tavernspite. Ignore the lane to your right to Gelli-Halog Quarries and proceed to the next road on your right.

17. (O.R.S) When you reach this road turn RIGHT and go up a slight hill, soon you will see some Power Pylons ahead of you. When the road bends to the left you will see to your RIGHT ahead of you a gate and a bridleway sign leading down a track.

18. Go through the gate and head down the rough track passing under the pylons. Pass through another gate onto a metalled road section to another gate at Trenewydd Farm. Ignoring the fork to your left, pass STRAIGHT on through this gate and pass in front of the farm house. Soon you will cross over a stream and follow the road bearing off to your right. Soon, you will come to the main A477 road.

19. (R.S.) At the main road, go STRAIGHT across following the sign to Colby Woodland Garden. This is a very busy road SO PLEASE TAKE CARE. Pass the little Baptist Church on your left and go down the hill with a view of the sea in front of you, to the T-junction.

20. At the T-junction turn RIGHT still following the signs to Colby Woodland Garden, carry on descending, passing Pendeilo Leisure Park on your right. Straight ahead there is a wonderful view of the sea and Caldey Island. Ignore the turning to your right to Colby Woodland Garden and carry on to the old church of Amroth.

21. Turn RIGHT at the church and go down the 1:6 hill. Take care.

22. At the bottom of the hill before the bridge turn RIGHT into the car park where you started your journey.

Amroth

Amroth is a pretty little seaside village at the start of the Pembrokeshire long distance coastal path. The land has undergone much erosion since prehistoric times, and sometimes at very low tide or after a storm it is possible to see the gnarled, twisted remains of a prehistoric forest.

In recent times Amroth has been very much at the mercy of the wild sea. Throughout the Autumn months the combination of high tides and gales has often caused serious damage to Amroth. It is for this reason that much development has not taken place. Prior to the storms of the 1930s there were cottages all along both sides of the road, but during the storms the buildings on the sea side of the road were destroyed by the sea. Appeals to the Government for a grant to build a new sea wall were refused and it was not until after the war that a new sea defence wall was built.

In the Autumn, when there is a severe easterly gale, many go down to Amroth and watch the sea launch huge boulders through the houses and shops remaining on the land side of the sea front road. We do not recommend that you ride your bike along here on these days!

Amroth beach

How was it for us?

Some days you feel full of energy and on others you can hardly make the effort to put your shoes on. This was one of the can't-put-your-shoes-on days. The sun was shining and the sky was a clear cloudless blue; England was playing Australia at Lords. I thought this was the day to sit in the garden, get a tan and listen to the cricket on the radio; Barbara my wife had other ideas. "Let's go for a bike ride," she demanded with that look in her eye that dares one to sit in the garden and be lazy. Ten minutes later, we had decided to get the bikes out of the garage and go for an easy ride.

Amroth is only a few miles from where we live but we lazily took the bikes on the car, to avoid the hill out of Wisemans Bridge, and parked in the village car park. The route was planned to avoid as many hills as possible and to stop at numerous watering holes on the way.

We cycled out of the car-park and turned left onto the coast road. A shimmer of heat was lifting skyward from the tarmac and on our right the waves lazily lapped at the edge of the sand. Because it was early in the holiday season only a few people were scattered along the strip of beach left by the encroaching tide. Across Carmarthen bay we could clearly see Rhossily and Worms Head tipped with a halo of white from the rolling surf. This is how cycling should always be, a long flat road, sun, no wind, beautiful company and wonderful scenery to look at.

All too soon we turned left off the coast road onto a bridleway that passed between two cottages and slowly started to climb away from the coast. On our left the hill climbed steeply and was shrouded in trees, to our right we had a wonderful view over the valley, the sea and Top Castle (an iron age fort) on Marros mountain.

The track started to swing left and get steeper until, on our right, we passed a track. This led to the ruin of an old disused factory which gave its name to the wood that we had just passed through. I have tried to find out from the locals what the building was used for, but so far I have had no success. At the turning to Trelessy Farm the track became metalled and levelled out to become a flat lane that led to the little village of Llanteglos.

In the village, we turned right at the T-junction and cycled on towards Llanteg. When we reached the village pond and a cross-roads we sped straight on, and soon we were at another cross-roads at the main A477 trunk road in Llanteg. For years we have passed this way driving on the main road to Carmarthen. We have always wanted to visit the medieval church of Crunwere, up on the hill, so we decided to make a detour. We crossed over the main road and entered the narrow lane that led up to the church. The church was set away from the road so we passed through a gate and crossed a field to reach it. On its own, away from any other dwellings, it seems a strange place to build a church. Maybe there was once a village here and it has slowly moved away due to changes in circumstance.

After visiting the church we rode back to the main road and took the lane to Tavernspite, and soon the road began to climb steeply. Considering that this was going to be an easy ride, this hill certainly made us out of breath. At the top of the hill we came to an old house called Crunwere House, several large oak trees stood in the garden filled with rooks screeching and squawking. The road started to descend so we both let go of the brakes and sped down the lane. After a while the road slowly started climbing again and soon after we passed under some power pylons and reached the road junction in Tavernspite.

Tavernspite cannot be called picturesque, but it does have a certain charm about it. Although many houses have been recklessly modernised, you can still see that they are quite old. We passed over the road junction and, with the village pump on our left, turned left into the main street. The Alpha Inn beckoned on our left but we rode on until we reached Tavernspite Garden Centre for this was to be our first port of call. In the café they make an excellent cup of tea and wonderful home-made cakes that seem even nicer after a hard climb on the bike.

Suitably refreshed we turned left out of the Garden Centre and took a right at the cross-roads. The view from here of the Preseli Mountains is wonderful and the colours an artist's dream, or a nightmare if you paint as I do. The road descended into the valley, and we free-wheeled to the T-junction and the old chapel which was built in 1797. Turning right at the road junction we rode through the wooded valley passing a large pond on our right where several fishermen were sitting enjoying the sun while they endeavoured to catch their supper.

The narrow lane twisted and turned and the high hedges blocked out the sun as we slowly climbed to another road junction. We turned left and followed the sign post to Narberth. This road was wider and almost flat, so we rode along enjoying the views of the country side. After crossing over an old stone bridge we entered Lampeter Velfrey. Today we were going to turn left at the cross-roads and give the village a miss, but if you want to go straight on the village centre is only a short distance away. In the village to your right is an extremely small church – the smallest we have ever seen. A few years ago while we were walking through Lampeter Velfrey we got talking to a woman who looked after this church, and she very kindly gave us a guided tour of this wonderful building; incidentally, the tour only lasted a few minutes.

The hill out of the village is quite steep and seems to go on for ever as it winds its way out of the valley. At Gilfach cross-roads we went straight on and, at last, the road started to descend. After passing a couple of roads to our left and right we reached another cross-roads at the B4314. Here we carried straight on and we passed on our right a large house called New House which is the source of Princess Gate Spring water. At a staggered cross-roads we turned left and rode on towards Tavernspite. Cycling along this straight lane, we ambled on until we took the second turning on our right. This lane climbed until we reached a bridleway on our right. We turned onto the bridleway passed through an iron field gate and went down a rough track. Halfway along the track we met a couple coming towards us; we stopped to let them pass and commented on what a lovely day it was. They told us they were from Holland on a hiking holiday; it was the first time they had visited Wales and Pembrokeshire and they said how much they had enjoyed it.

Time was passing fast so we said our farewells and continued on the bridleway, passed through Trenewydd Farm and then cycled on a rough track until we reached the main A477 road. At the main road we went straight across into a lane that headed back towards Amroth. To out left were wonderful views of the sea and in the distance Tenby and Caldy Island. The flat road suddenly started to descend and as we forked right by the old Amroth parish church the road plunged down towards the sea. This road really was steep and we had to hold on tight to our brakes to stop from hurtling down the hill. Suddenly we were at the right turning into the car park where we had started our journey. It had been a pleasant ride on a wonderful summer's day and anyway England, as usual, had a bad day in the Test match.

Ride 2: Saundersfoot, Templeton, Ludchurch, Saundersfoot

Abbreviations: O.R.S. Off-road Section; R.S. Road Section.

Distance: 17 miles.

Time: 3 hours.

Terrain: Country lanes, bridleways. Two climbs. Moderate.

Maps Required: Outdoor Leisure 35, South Pembrokeshire.

Start: At the Regency car park Saundersfoot. Grid Reference 137 048.

1. Leave the car park by the entrance and pass the toilet block on your right. Just before you come to the road, which is the one-way system through the village, you will see a small lane to your LEFT signposted "Brooklands Place, Private Road". Proceed along this lane to the road (the route of an old railway to Bonvilles Court Colliery).

2. (O.R.S) At Westfield Road turn LEFT and ride onwards until the road you are on takes a sharp left turn up a steep hill. Do not climb this hill but go STRAIGHT ahead onto a newly metalled track passing Incline Cottage on your right. After about a quarter of a mile you will pass the Waterworks on your left.

3. Keep STRAIGHT on and climb a steep hill on an old sunken roadway until you reach an old lane to your right.

4. Turn RIGHT into the old lane and carry on to a T-junction.

5. (R.S) At the T-junction turn RIGHT up the hill to another T-junction (The Ridgeway)

6. At this T-junction turn LEFT.

7. When you reach the next T-junction turn RIGHT.

8. Carry on down the hill and pass Netherwood School on your right then take the first turning on your LEFT. On your right you will see the old church of St Issell's through the trees.

9. Climb up Errox Hill and then go down the hill and pass under the railway bridge.

10. Just past the railway bridge turn RIGHT down a footpath running via a subway under the new by-pass. Continue to the T-junction in Killgetty by the White Horse pub.

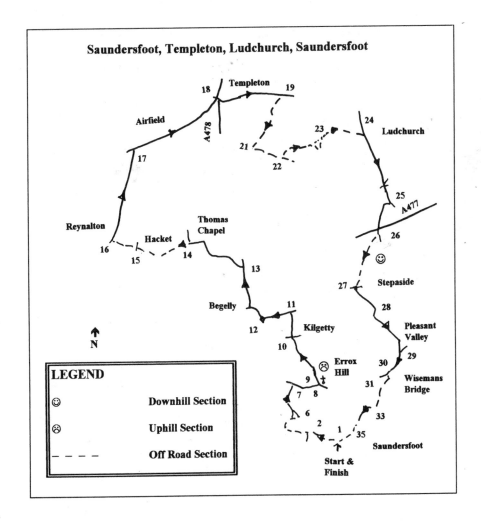

11. At this T-junction turn LEFT. Ride along the old main Carmarthen road, pass Leo's Store on your left, until you reach a roundabout.

12. At the roundabout turn RIGHT onto the A478, climb the hill and pass Begelly Church on your left. Ignore the road on your left. Carry on for about ½ mile until you come to a shop and petrol pumps on your left.

13. Just past the shop, turn LEFT into a lane signposted to Thomas Chapel. Keep on this lane passing Moorland Farm on your left, look out for the little pigs on the wall of the house. Ride on to Thomas Chapel; here the lane takes a sharp right turn. At this point, turn LEFT and skirt to the RIGHT of the village pond. Ignore the track to your left but keep STRAIGHT on past the bungalows on your left and your right.

14. (O.R.S) Keep STRAIGHT on down a narrow old lane and pass an old cottage on your left. Cross over the stream and climb the hill on a rough track to the road at Hackett.

15. At the road, go STRAIGHT on and continue down another rough lane. Cross over another stream and cycle on to the road at Reynalton.

16. (R.S.) Turn RIGHT and continue, ignoring the road to your right and with Church Lands Farm on your left, to a T-junction by an old Airfield.

17. At the T-junction turn RIGHT and carry on this road, climb the hill and pass the two radio masts on your left. Ignore the road to your right. Go down the hill to the cross-roads by the Boars Head pub in Templeton. (This is a five-way junction)

18. At the cross-roads go STRAIGHT over; this has a slight left stagger. Go down this lane passing under a railway bridge to Ludchurch (do not go up the hill into Templeton on the A478). Carry on up the hill and pass Springfield House on your right. When you reach Chapel Hill Farm and the Z bend sign on your left continue for a few metres. Just before the sharp right-hand bend in the road you will see on your right a metal gate and a bridleway sign.

19. (O.R.S) At this point, where there is also a sign to Rowston Farm, turn RIGHT and go through a gate onto a bumpy bridleway. Keep on the bridleway, then fork RIGHT to an iron gate. Pass through this gate and climb a hill across an open field, heading for the gate STRAIGHT ahead. Go through this gate and head for another gate to the left of the field by a wood. Grid reference 120 106.

20. Pass through this gate and enter Simpson Hill Wood. Within a few metres, at a track T-junction turn RIGHT. Go down the hill to a wide track on your left.

21. At this track turn LEFT and climb up a slight hill. Keep on this track, ignore the track on your left and cycle on to a track coming up a hill from your right.

22. At this junction turn LEFT and keep on this track, ignoring tracks to your left and right. Climb up a slight hill and you will come into a cleared wood at a track cross-roads (not shown as such on the map).

23. Turn LEFT and, within a few metres at a track T-junction, turn RIGHT. You can see the spire of Ludchurch Church in the distance in front of you. Carry on and pass through a wooden gate and a metal gate. Soon you will reach a metalled road which, within thirty metres, becomes gravelled; bear RIGHT here and ride down this lane passing through Roadside Farm at grid reference 137 107 to a T-junction in Ludchurch.

24. (R.S) At the T-junction turn RIGHT. Go down the hill ignoring the roads to your right and to your left. Climb up a hill to a left-hand bend by Little Kings Park Caravan Site.

25. At the caravan site turn RIGHT into a narrow lane, signposted "No Through Road'. Go down a hill to a gate across the road at Bangeston House. Go through the gate. Be very careful: this is the main A477 by-pass – PLEASE TAKE CARE when crossing.

26. (O.R.S.) At the main road go STRAIGHT across, down a narrow lane (this is a right-hand stagger.) At the houses bear RIGHT up the hill along an old green lane. Soon the old lane starts to descend to a T-junction in Stepaside.

27. (R.S.) At the T-junction turn RIGHT, go down the hill and quickly turn RIGHT by the main road following the signpost to Wisemans Bridge. Pass Stepaside Coach works on your right.

28. Within a few metres turn LEFT and pass under a road bridge into Pleasant Valley.

29. Carry on the road through Pleasant Valley. Climb the hill and at the T-junction turn RIGHT onto the coast road. Pass the Wisemans Bridge Inn on your left and pass over Wisemans River Bridge.

30. Just past the bridge turn LEFT onto a track running beside the sea.

31. (O.R.S) Continue along the coast track through two old railway tunnels until you come to Coppet Hall car park. Please take care along this section, especially through the tunnels. ALWAYS GIVE WAY TO PEOPLE WALKING.

32. Cross over the car park and head for a tunnel and toilet block in the south corner of the car park.

33. Go through the tunnel and you will come to The Strand road going through Saundersfoot. Keep on the road until you reach the cross-roads.

34. At the cross-roads turn LEFT, keeping the Cambrian Hotel on your right.

35. Bear RIGHT, and follow the one-way system, passing the amusement arcade on your left. You are soon back at the car park where you started your journey

Saundersfoot

Saundersfoot is renowned for its beautiful sandy beaches and picturesque harbour. The harbour however owes its origin to earlier days when it was constructed for the boats to carry coal from the nearby coalfield. It is hard to imagine that this tranquil, pretty little harbour ever had a less attractive past, for nothing remains to indicate its industrial heritage. There are many yachts, pleasure boats and fishing boats in the harbour and it is now a very pleasant place to sail, fish or just to sit around and watch the world go by.

The ride takes you along the Strand which was earlier known as Railway Street, for it was along here that the colliery train ran. The tunnels remain and form part of the path to Wisemans Bridge. The existence of the railway led to the growth of other industries in the area. A brick works was founded at Wisemans Bridge and there was also an iron foundry at Stepaside. In the cliffs at the side of the Wisemans Bridge path you will see the remains of iron ore seams. These industries however only lasted for about 30 years, due to the remoteness of the area and the fall in the price of pig iron. The remains of the foundry can be seen on your return at point 27. They are very picturesque in their ruined state.

Saundersfoot

St Issell's Church

St Issell's is a charming church set in the most tranquil of surround-
ings. It has a fortified tower, which in earlier days was used as a
lookout tower in the days of conflict between the English-speaking
locals and the Welsh-speaking North Pembrokeshire people.

Begelly

Begelly Parish Church is a 13th/14th century building. The church
was restored in 1886 and a bell cast in Bridgewater was added to the
battlemented tower. Below the church stood an earthwork castle of
the Norman Lord of the manor of Begelly. Only a few irregular
mounds can be seen, because the castle was destroyed to make way
for a graveyard extension.

Templeton

The place name of Templeton owes its origin to the Knights Tem-
plar, the powerful military brethren formed to protect pilgrims on
their hazardous journeys. It was here that a church or hospice was
built, but alas nothing remains of this once important building.
Many cottages in this village are of Medieval origin with lateral
chimneys, but you have to look hard to see the antiquity due to
foolish modernisation during the past few years.

Ludchurch

Ludchurch Medieval church is a fine building, perched on an
outcrop of rock left behind after quarrying for limestone in the 18th
century. Beside the entrance door is a holy water stoup carved in
the shape of a human head; more pagan-looking heads adorn the
capitals of the aisle arcade. The church, built around the 13th to
14th centuries, has a simple chancel, a nave and a 15th century
tower. The first recorded rector was John de Augers in 1381. In the
churchyard is the tomb of Judge Wilfred Bough Allen who was
married to the grand-daughter of Josiah Wedgwood the famous
pottery maker. Here also you will discover the grave of Captain John

Martin who was the navigator to Captain Cook on his famous voyages of discovery to Australia and the Pacific.

How was it for us?

Most tourists visiting Pembrokeshire stay within the vicinity of the busy seaside towns of Tenby and Saundersfoot. We have added this ride so that those people, and locals with mountain bikes, can get away from it all and discover the hidden countryside just a stone's throw away from the hustle and bustle of these towns. Most of this trip takes you down quiet country lanes, ancient bridleways and long-forgotten railway tracks. Other than the main holiday months of July and August you will be surprised to find you have these routes almost to yourself.

Maybe I'm biased because I live in Saundersfoot, but the countryside and the seashore around this area are simply beautiful at any time of the year. Since the first time I discovered this ride, I have ridden it often in Spring, Summer, Autumn and Winter; there is always something different to see and experience.

The ride I am going to write about took place on a very warm Saturday in August. The roads were busy due to the many tourists coming and going, so we decided that it was time to try a local ride. Out came the map, I planned a route and off we went.

We set off from the Regency car park in the centre of Saundersfoot and turned left into Brooklands Place. This narrow lane was once the route of the old railway that ran to Bonvilles Court Colliery. The six of us rode along this flat lane chatting and enjoying the warm sunshine. When we reached Westfield Road we turned left and cycled on until the road turned sharp left up a steep hill, but we headed straight on along the old lane with the stream on our right. Soon we passed the waterworks on our left at which point the lane became rough and started to climb steeply. The surface of this sunken green lane is made of old stones that have been there for hundreds of years. They are smooth and slippery, and it took all our skill and strength to negotiate this section.

At the top of the hill we turned right down another track and rode on past the site of Bonvilles Court Colliery – not that you would guess that it ever existed today – until we reached a T-junction. We turned right and then left, and were on Fan Road – named after the ruined building of the colliery fan that can just be seen through a jungle of trees on the right-hand side of the road. When we reached the next T-junction we turned right and headed down the hill, with the sea glinting in the distance through the trees. We passed Netherwood School and just after the school we took a sharp left turn. With St Issell's church on our right we started to climb Erroxs Hill. It doesn't matter how often I have cycled up this hill, it always seems to nearly burst my lungs and I am always grateful to reach the left-hand bend that tells me I'm at the top.

We went down the lane and passed under the railway bridge. Immediately after the bridge we turned right and walked under the subway that passed under the new Kilgetty by-pass. At the lane we turned left and cycled on until we reached the T-junction in Kilgetty by the White Horse Inn. Here we turned left and rode down the old main road through the village, which is free of traffic since the by-pass was built in 1983. When we reached the roundabout we turned right and cycled along the main road towards Narberth, passing Begelly Church on our left. Luckily this section of the main road is quite short. It was only minutes before we were passing the shop and garage on our left and turning left into a quiet lane on our way to Thomas Chapel.

Between high hedges of foxgloves and blackberries we meandered along the almost flat lane until we reached the few hamlets that make up Thomas Chapel. The road took a sharp right-hand turn, but we turned left, and with the village pond on our left, we cycled down an old green lane. The lane soon became rough and stony and soon we came to the first stream that we had to ford. We splashed through the water and slogged up the steep stony track; the August growth of brambles hung across the path like a thousand needles. It was here that we wished we were wearing long track bottoms rather than our cycle shorts. Inside 100m the track became wider; the surface flatter and grassy, and soon we reached the road at Hackett Farm.

Opposite, there was another narrow track and so we crossed the road and headed down between the high hedgerows. Soon the track dipped into a gully and crossed over a stream and as we cycled up the track huge divots of mud were flung into the air from our back tyres. Everyone jostled to pass to avoid getting an eyeful. The track wandered along through the trees; the surface hard and compact, until it emerged at the road in Reynalton.

Six children were playing cricket on the road and they were surprised to see us emerge from this little-used track. In order for us to pass they grudgingly moved the wooden box that they were using for a wicket, and gave us withering looks for disturbing their game. As we turned right and rode on up the road, the game was resumed with the passion of the England v Australia Test Match.

Without the shade of the trees we rode along the straight lane in blistering heat. Gently the lane climbed up towards the old disused Templeton airfield, and at the T-junction we turned right and cycled on passing the two radio masts on our left. Soon the road descended to Templeton and the Boars Head Inn at the five-way road junction. Dehydration was starting to set in so we needed no excuse to stop and have a long cool drink at the Inn before we continued with our journey.

Thirty minutes later, refreshed and rested, we carried on across the cross-roads, passed under the very tall railway bridge and cycled on up the lane. Just after we passed the turning to Chapel Hill Farm on our left we turned right, through an iron field gate onto a rough bridleway. This track started to descend and become very bumpy. As we speeded up it seemed as if our bicycles had transformed into pneumatic drills that were shaking our teeth out. The track took a couple of turns and we came to another field gate that led into an open field. Across the field in the distance we could make out the woods and the next gate that we were heading for. We set off across the field. Half way across a herd of young Heifers came curiously galloping up to see what we were doing. The girls, who do not like cattle of any description, saw them coming and set off for the distant gate with legs pumping like mad and made it there in record time.

After passing through the gate into the forest of pine trees, we turned right and followed a wide path that descended slowly. As we rode along our bike wheels crushed the deep carpet of needles that littered the floor, sending skyward a wonderful aroma. Shafts of sunlight penetrated through the trees causing the light to flicker like an old silent movie. Soon we came to a wide almost flat track on our left, which we turned into and cycled along in sheer delight. At a cross-roads of tracks we turned left and rode out of the forest into bright sunlight. Here the trees had been felled for timber and after the cool of the forest the day seemed hot and oppressive. Straight ahead in the distance we could make out our destination, the church spire of Ludchurch so we followed the track in that direction.

When we reached the road at Ludchurch we decided to make a detour and visit the lakes made by the old quarry workings. We also wanted to look at the old church. First we sat by the lake and indulged in a welcome picnic of crisps and ham sandwiches washed down with orange squash. This was a lovely spot to spend a hot sunny afternoon. As we sat relaxing a gaggle of ducks swam to us over the ripple-less lake. They paraded up and down before us quacking for pieces of bread and crisps. Ludchurch church is set upon an outcrop of rock which was left standing there like a pillar of salt by the old quarrying that removed the surrounding stone. We walked around the graveyard looking for the graves of the famous people who were buried there and then, as the evening was drawing nigh we decided that it was time to finish our journey.

With reluctance we set off down the lane, crossing straight over the cross-roads and climbing the hill until we reached a caravan site. We turned right and cycled down a narrow lane until we reached a wooden gate that blocked the road. After passing through the gate we came to the main Carmarthen to Pembroke trunk road. Luckily we could see for miles in both directions, so when we saw a gap in the Saturday traffic we scampered across to the lane opposite. This old green lane, named the Farmers Road by the locals, soon became rough and overgrown as it stretched across the parched golden Summer fields. Soon we were cycling between high hedges that hadn't been cut for so many years that they blotted out the sun. When we reached the cottages we turned right down the steep hill and took a right and a left and passed under the road bridge into Pleasant Valley.

How aptly named is this pleasant wooded lane that runs beside the stream to Wisemans Bridge, with its old water mill and Pembrokeshire cottages. We ambled along enjoying the evening sun; even the short hill up to the coast road didn't unduly spoil our enjoyment. Here we turned right and sped down the road, passing the Wisemans Bridge Inn on our left. The sea came into sight and the wonderful view of Saundersfoot and Monkstone Point. The sea was a beautiful cobalt blue and the surface was dotted with yachts with sails of red and white.

After crossing over the old bridge we turned left onto the old railway track that runs alongside the cliffs to Saundersfoot. Negotiating our way down the two dark railway tunnels we at last emerged into the sunshine at Coppet Hall car park. Crossing over the car park, we entered another tunnel to emerge on the road in Saundersfoot. We rode through the village, went around the one-way system and turned left into the car park where we had started our journey. It had been a pleasant and enjoyable ride and so to end the day we headed for Tiffer's ice-cream shop on the slipway to devour the biggest, creamiest ice-cream we could afford.

Ride 3: Canaston wood, Minwear, Narberth

Abbreviations: O.R.S. Off-road Section; R.S. Road Section.

Distance: 20 miles.

Time: 4 hours.

Terrain: Country lanes and Bridleways

Grade: Can be difficult in wet weather.

Map: Ordnance Survey Outdoor Leisure 36, South Pembrokeshire.

Start and Finish at Picnic Site by Minwear Wood, ½ mile south-west of Blackpool Mill. Grid Reference 085 138.

1. (R.S.) With the Picnic Site at your back turn RIGHT onto the road, and ride on to the turning on your right to Minwear Farm and Minwear Medieval Church. This is well worth a visit.

2. (O.R.S.) Nearly opposite the road on your right turn LEFT through a gate into a narrow bridleway. Follow this, passing through three gates to a T-junction at a metalled road (in wet weather this bridleway becomes very muddy).

3. Turn RIGHT and ride along this lane passing the horse centre on your left to a T-junction.

4. Go STRAIGHT across at the T-junction (slight right stagger) through a gate onto a Permissive Path. Keep STRAIGHT on through the gates across the fields to the road at Highgate Farm.

5. When you reach the T-junction turn RIGHT. Soon after you go around the left-hand bend at Flimston Farm the road becomes unsurfaced. Ride on to the fork in the track and fork RIGHT (the left-hand fork goes to Knapps Farm). Go down into the valley, here the track can be very muddy in places. Climb to the top of the hill to a lane on your left.

6. (R.S.) Turn LEFT into the lane and ride on to a T-junction at Yerbeston.

7. Turn LEFT at the T-junction and climb up the hill to the cross-roads at the main A4075.

8. Proceed STRAIGHT on at the cross-roads. Soon you will be at another cross-roads at the B4586 where you again go STRAIGHT on.

9. Ride on down the hill and cross over Carne Bridge and climb up out of the valley. Ride on ignoring the road to your left to a road to your right to Reynalton.

10. (O.R.S.) Turn LEFT and go through a gate on to a bridleway that crosses an old airfield. Go STRAIGHT across the air field to the gate at the main A4115 road. This track is confusing as there are old runways running in all directions, but try and make your way as best that you can.

11. Go STRAIGHT across at the main road into the bridleway opposite, passing a house on your left. Ride along the bridleway through Little Molleston wood on your left, to a cross-roads.

12. Go STRAIGHT on at the cross-roads on to another bridleway and ride on to a T-junction of bridleways where you turn LEFT.

13. Soon you again come to another track cross-roads. At Pitch Cross, turn RIGHT, marked as a bridleway on the map. Cycle along this lane to some houses and the main A478 road to Narberth.

14. Turn LEFT onto the main road and then turn RIGHT onto another bridleway at Woods Cross. Proceed along this lane to a cross-roads.

15. At the cross-roads go STRAIGHT on down yet another rough lane. Go down into the valley, and at the bottom of the hill, at a track T-junction turn LEFT.

16. Proceed along this track with the river on your right to a cross-roads at the main A478 at Narberth Bridge. Go STRAIGHT on at the cross-roads.

17. (R.S.) Ride on along this lane, and soon, at the fork in the road go RIGHT and proceed to a very sharp right-hand bend, a distance of about 2 miles.

18. (O.R.S.) At the bend turn LEFT onto a narrow rough and steep bridleway that runs into the woods. Follow this narrow track to a wider track crossing your path.

19. Turn RIGHT and go down the hill. Cross over the ford and climb up the hill to the main A4075 road.

20. Go STRAIGHT on at the main road on to the bridleway opposite and descend through the woods to a T-junction.

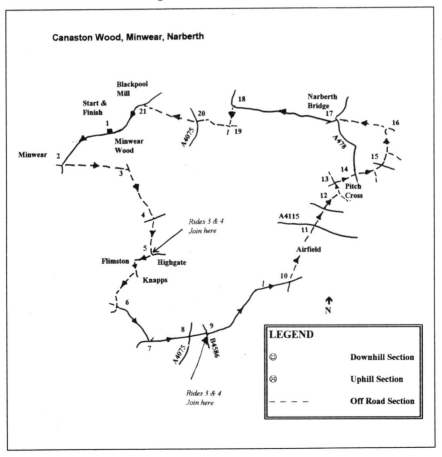

21. (R.S.) Turn LEFT at the T-junction, ride on passing Blackpool Mill (which can be seen working in the Summer) on your right. Carry on up the hill to the picnic site on your RIGHT where you started your journey.

Minwear

The original Minwear church was built in the 12th century, for the Manor of Minwear was granted in 1150 to the Order of the Knights Hospitallers, whose commandery lay across the river at Slebech. With its round headed doorway and its pierced low arches the church is in complete contrast to most other local churches. The Norman font has four heads carved on its side, but years of misuse as the local horse trough have taken their toll.

Narberth

This town mentioned in the Welsh folk tales of 'The Mabinogion' has a strange lost-in-time air about it. The Norman castle, or all that remains of it, sits on a hill on the edge of town and is thought to be built in the 12th century. A castle has stood here since 1116 when the Welsh besieged and captured the town and castle. After many battles especially in 1257 the existing stonework was added. "Some way must be used to keep out whose cursed Welsh." This was once a magnificent building with five towers, a great hall, kitchen, gallery and a great chamber, and a twin-towered gatehouse. Today, little remains apart from the two corner towers and a fragment of the keep and hall.

Blackpool Mill

Built in stone in 1813 by Baron De Rutzen of Slebech Hall. The corn mill is one of Britain's finest remaining examples of water driven machinery.

How was it for us?

This ride has been undertaken twice, both times in November but a year apart, and each time the ground has been wet and muddy. This hasn't detracted from

Blackpool Mill

the ride, far from it; the journey just became more fun. The route follows the old Knights Templars way that was used for hundreds of years and has changed very little since Medieval times. All of the bridleways pass through either pretty woodland or scenic open fields.

So on a damp Saturday in November the six of us set out from Minwear picnic site. The air was still and damp with the early morning mist hanging in the trees. Not a cold day, just one of those days when the dampness gets through to your bones. From the picnic site the road slowly descends so it wasn't hard to move along at a fast pace for the first couple of miles. Soon we were at our first turning left, into a narrow bridleway. The hard work began. The track was narrow and very muddy and with every turn of the wheels you sank into the mire. It took all our strength to plough our way slowly along, dodging the deep puddles and weaving in and out of the tree roots that have grown across the path. We were soon covered in mud from head to toe, and it was a picture seeing Jill and Barbara's usually well-made-up faces splattered in mud – so if mud improves the complexion no one in this party will have any spots for a long time.

At the end of the bridleway we turned right into a narrow lane and cycled along an almost flat section, until we reached a road. Here we headed straight across onto a permissive path that went through a gate and crossed over three open fields. In the last field a herd of young Heifers decided that we looked interesting, so we decided to make a quick escape. At the next bridleway we turned right and after passing Flimston Farm descended into the valley, where we had to ford a large puddle that had spread itself across the track. The bikes all needed the mud washing, so we just headed through. After the water splash we climbed up the hill and turned left into a narrow lane.

The lane soon led us to Yerbeston where we turned left and climbed the steep hill up to the main road. We crossed straight over the main road and then, after another cross-roads, descended a steep hill to Carne Bridge. The road started a slight climb through a pretty wood until we reached the right turning to Reynalton.

Here we turned left through a gate onto a bridle-path that according to the map heads straight across the old disused airfield. To find this bridle-path on the ground is no mean feat, for there is no sign that it has ever existed. So we did exactly what we did the first time that we completed this journey, which was to follow the old runways heading in the correct direction. It really was strange to be able to ride six abreast. With a few twists and a few turns we were soon at the road opposite the next bridleway. We decided that it was time for lunch, so we found a sheltered spot with some grass to sit on and devoured our welcome provisions.

With our bellies full we set off across the road and entered the narrow bridleway, here the track was stony but it had a good surface so we made good time. Very soon we crossed another road and entered a bridleway that was rougher and wetter; The going got a little harder as the track started to climb. At the end of the track we hit our first problem; Ben had a puncture, so with muddy hands we all mucked in (literally) to get it repaired; Tom found that he had a flat too, so it was off with the wheel and repair Tom's bike as well. With all our problems solved we set off with renewed vigour, but within 200m John also had a flat tyre – maybe it was the thorn bushes on the last track, but we had lost at least half an hour.

We continued, crossed the main Narberth road and started to plunge down a rough track into a valley. Here the track was rutted and leaves hid the ground under your wheels, making it extremely difficult to select the correct line, but John, the two boys, and myself sent caution to the wind and sped to the bottom on a switch-back ride of our lifetime. At the bottom we waited by the river while the girls gingerly walked down the steep track.

The track followed alongside the river. Up on the hill, to our right, stood the forlorn ruin of Narberth Castle, its crumbling tower leaning like a drunken man. When we reached the road at Narberth Bridge we went straight across and for the first time since we left the airfield we cycled on a metalled surface. As we sped along, the mud that was caked into our tyres shot into the air, making every one race to be in front so they didn't get an eye-full. The road section lasted for about two miles and we turned left through a narrow gate onto another bridleway that headed into Canaston Wood.

This track was narrow and climbed into the wood and as we had lost so much time because of the punctures it was starting to get dark. We scrambled along the track, pushing our bikes over the difficult terrain, but this section was only short and we soon hit the main track running across our path. It was here that John realised why he was having so much trouble seeing where he was going, he still had his dark sunglasses on!

From this point we turned right and headed down the hill speeding through the trees and across the ford. Soon we hit a short hill that we climbed until we reached the main road. Here we went straight across onto another bridleway that plunged again through the woods until we reached the lane by Blackpool Mill. Our journey was nearly over, so we turned left and climbed breathlessly up the steep hill to the picnic site where we had started our journey.

Ride 4: Carew Castle, Loveston, Yerbeston, Martletwy, Lawrenny

Abbreviations: O.R.S. Off-road Section; R.S. Road Section.

Distance: 22 miles.

Time: 3 – 4 hours.

Terrain: Lanes and bridle paths. No really steep hills but three very muddy sections. Moderate.

Map: Outdoor Leisure 36 South Pembrokeshire.

Start and Finish: At the picnic site north of Carew Castle Just off the main A4075. Grid Reference 042 039.

1. Turn LEFT out of the picnic site and take the first road on your RIGHT.

2. Ride on through Carew Newton, ignoring the lane to your right. Carry on to a T-junction.

3. At the T-junction turn RIGHT and cycle on to a cross-roads.

4. When you reach the cross-roads turn LEFT and go down to Cresswell Quay. On the right is the old Cresselly Inn which is well worth a stop. If you don't stop now, you will pass the Inn again at the end of your journey, so by then you might need a pint of amber nectar to help you finish your ride. Ride on and ignore the two roads to your right and cross over the old Cresswell Bridge. Soon you will reach a road forking off to your left. Take the RIGHT fork, and quite soon you will reach a lane on your right signposted as a bridleway.

5. Turn RIGHT and follow the lane marked as a bridleway and also waymarked as the Landsker Borderlands Trail. Pass Cresswell Farm on your left, go through a gate and go down the hill – the track becomes rough and muddy. Carry on up this track and cross over a stream. We would advise you to cross over the bridge, as the stream is quite deep. On the other side of the stream pass through another muddy section and climb up a hill; keep on to a gate by Thorn Farm. Go through this gate and follow the way marks to the T-junction at the main road A4075.

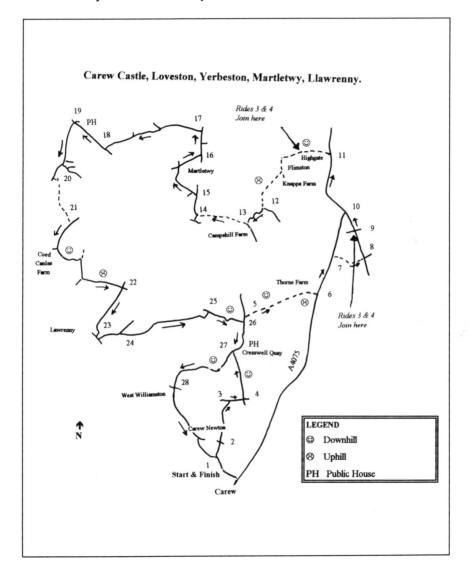

Carew Castle, Loveston, Yerbeston, Martletwy, Llawrenny.

6. (R.S.) When you are at the main road turn LEFT and keep on this road for about a mile until just before Halfway House. Look out for a bridleway signpost on your RIGHT.

7. (O.R.S.) Turn RIGHT at the bridleway. Go through the gate into the field and head straight across the field to the gate and the way-mark in the far left-hand corner. Go through this gate and head down a narrow winding path to another gate on a steep slope. Pass through the gate and follow the path that winds to your right over marsh land. Head up a slight hill and pass through another gate onto a wider track. Follow this track to the houses at the cross-roads.

8. (R.S.) At the cross-roads turn LEFT and go down the hill. Climb up the hill and pass Loveston School on your left. Carry on to the cross-roads.

9. At the cross-roads, go STRAIGHT on, and cycle on to the A4075 main road.

10. At the main road turn RIGHT. This isn't a very busy road but take care. Pass Hungerford Farm on your right, within about a mile you will see a lane to your left marked as a bridleway.

11. (O.R.S.) Turn LEFT into the bridleway and proceed on past Highgate Farm on your left. When you reach Flimston Farm the lane turns LEFT and becomes unsurfaced. Follow this track to Knapps Farm, where the track turns sharp right and goes down a hill. At the bottom of the hill the track becomes wet and muddy in places. Climb up the hill out of the valley. At the top of the hill the track becomes a metalled road and you come to a lane approaching from your left.

12. Branch RIGHT, carry on along the lane until you see a gate and a bridleway to your right. If you reach Campshill Farm you have gone too far.

13. Turn RIGHT through the gate and follow the bridleway across the fields, heading for the gate straight ahead of you. Pass through this gate into the next field. Don't take the track that turns left, but head STRAIGHT on in a westerly direction towards the wood. Soon you will see a way mark post and a path heading into the wood. Follow the path that winds down into the wood, go through a gate and cross over a stream. The day we did the ride, everybody elected to ride through the stream rather than cross over the bridge, but beware, Barbara didn't quite make it and got a ducking. After the stream the path climbs up a hill and passes through another gate into a field. Carry on up the field towards a farm and the gate that you can see ahead of you. Pass through the gate by the derelict Waddock Farm and carry on to the road.

14. (R.S.) At the road turn RIGHT and cycle along to the first lane on your left, signposted 'To The Vineyard'.

15. Turn LEFT into the lane and head for Martletwy village. Pass through the village and at the T-junction by Post Office Cottage turn RIGHT. Pass the picnic site on your left, or stop and have a bite to eat. Climb up the hill and bear left following the signpost to Cross Hands.

16. Within a few hundred metres the road bears right, but here you turn LEFT down a smaller lane following the signpost to Landshipping.

17. Soon after take the first turning LEFT, again signposted to Landshipping, and carry on down this lane passing through Whitlow Farm to a road from your left, near to a telephone box.

18. Bear RIGHT and head down towards the river and the Stanley Arms on your right, where it's well worth a stop for a cooling drink, or two.

19. After your drink or drinks, carry on and bear left by the river. Follow on round Landshipping Quay and bear RIGHT along a road (marked on the map as a permissive road) with the river on your right.

20. (O.R.S.) Soon you will reach a wood on your left. Look out for a yellow way marked Footpath to your left entering into the wood. Turn LEFT onto the narrow footpath and follow the yellow way marks through the wood to an opening into a field. This is a detour not marked on the map, but it by-passes around Wood House to connect with the original road used as a footpath on the map. Go into the field and then turn left and follow around the edge of the field, following the footpath signs to a gate. Pass through the gate and follow a muddy track to the road at a T-junction by Broadley Farm.

21. (R.S.) At this T-junction turn RIGHT, and head on, ignoring the lane to your right. Pass by Coedcanlas Farm and look out for the beautiful view on your right, out over the river. Go downhill and pass the remains of St Mary's Church on your right. Head up the hill to the cross-roads.

22. Turn RIGHT at the cross-roads and head on to Garron's Pill; here you can stop and look out across the river to Beggars Reach and Benton Wood on the other side. Carry on, climb up the hill and keep on to Lawrenny, passing the old church of Lawrenny on your right

23. Just past the church, take the LEFT fork and carry on through the village passing the cricket club on your right.

24. Soon take the next RIGHT fork down a narrow lane and continue, passing through Lawrenny Newton Farm to a T-junction.

25. At the T-junction turn RIGHT. Pass Little Pencoed on your left and go down the hill to the next T-junction.

26. When you are at the T-junction turn RIGHT and head back across Cresswell Bridge and ride on passing Cresselly Inn on your left. At this point you might well need that drink! Climb up the hill and as you go round the left-hand bend fork RIGHT into a narrow lane.

27. Go down into the valley with a wonderful view out over the river on your right. Ignore the road on your left and continue to West Williamston.

28. In the village you come to a cross-roads; go STRAIGHT on (slight left fork). Ignore all roads to your right and left and cycle on to the picnic site on your RIGHT where you started your journey.

Variations

Rides 3 (Canaston Woods) & Ride 4 (Carew Castle) can be joined to make a ride of about 40 miles:

A. Start ride 4 at Carew Castle picnic site and follow instructions 1 to 9, at this cross-roads (B4586) you turn RIGHT.

B. You now connect with ride 3 and follow instructions 9 to 21 and then 1 to 5 (at Flimston Farm).

C. From Flimston Farm, follow ride 4 – instructions 11 to 28, and end at Carew Castle picnic site.

Carew Castle

Gerald of Windsor is reputed to have founded Carew at the beginning of the 12th century. Nothing above ground remains of the early castle but archaeologists have discovered a Norman bread oven and a silver penny of King Steven (1135-54). Evidence has also been obtained of a previous large Iron Age settlement on the site.

Carew Castle

It was in 1311 that Sir Nicholas de Carew rebuilt the castle with a large polygonal enclosure bristling with defensive towers of various shapes, also the Great and Lesser Halls were added at this time. In 1480 Sir Edmund Carew plunged himself into debt to refurbish the castle as one of the "Best houses in the land" by adding large windows and lavish residential chambers.

In the late 1500s Sir John Perrot was given governorship of Carew and he proceeded to turn the castle into an Elizabethan country house. A new range of buildings was established on the north side of the castle with tall mullioned windows, projecting oriel turrets and sham battlements. This is the striking and beautiful part of the castle viewed from across the river. Perrot never finished his alterations because he died before the feat could be accomplished. An inventory after his death mentions "so much glasse ready to be sett upp as will grace all the windowes of ye newe buildinge."

The castle was lived in until the Civil War, when in 1644 when it was used as a Royalist stronghold, it was taken by the Parliamentarian army and partially demolished.

The building is now the home of several species of bats, the most important being the protected greater horseshoe bat. The walls of the castle are also the habitat of many rare ferns and plants. The site is designated as both a Special Area of Conservation and a Site of Special Scientific Interest.

The castle is leased by the Pembrokeshire Coast National Park and is open to the public. During the Summer months there are special events, such as re-enactment of battles, jousting and demonstrations of activities relating to life in the castle.

Cresswell

Cresswell Quay is a beautiful little village with its pub and old stone quay set on the bank of the upper reaches of the Cleddau.

The old pub, known as the Cresselly Arms was built in 1576 and is an interesting example of an old stone built Tudor style building. This pub is a welcome watering place for locals and tourists alike because it still sells Real Ale. There is usually a selection of four different ales, although the landlord tells me that there may only be three choices in the winter. The building is said to be haunted by the ghost of a young girl who was drowned in the quay opposite.

Across the river on the heavily wooded bank can be glimpsed Cresswell Castle – a lesser-known example of a 15th century upper class fortified house. Built in 1540 by William Barlow, Bishop of St David's, it was lived in until the late 17th century. All that remains of this once lavish house is a dovecote and an oblong enclosure with four towers. Nearby are the ruins of a building believed to have been a chapel, and a holy well. It is from this holy well – Christ's Well – that the name Cresswell originated.

St Caradoc's Church, Lawrenny and Lawrenny Castle

St Caradoc's church is a magnificent 12th Century church with a four-storey tower, situated in Lawrenny. The south transept was added in the 14th or 15th centuries to house the stone effigy of a knight. The effigy was later moved and the tomb of Hugh Barlow put in its place. It is well worth a visit to see the Reredos Tapestry, worked by Mrs Patrick Lort-Phillips, which tells the story of St Caradog, and the beautiful stained glass window presented by Maude Lort-Phillips. The Lort-Phillips were local gentry who lived in Lawrenny Castle which is, sadly, demolished. Lawrenny Castle was built in 1856 at a cost of £70,000 and was demolished in 1952 because it was too expensive to run and no one wanted to buy it. The wooded drive that led up to the castle is now Lawrenny picnic site. If you ride into here you may notice that there is only one lion gracing the entrance, the other was stolen in the 1960s. Please leave the other one there!

How was it for us?

We have been on this ride or parts of it many times, and still never tire of the experience. The scenery across the river is simply breathtaking and Carew Castle must be one of the most scenic castles in the British Isles. It is also a good excuse to visit our favourite pub, the old Cresselly Inn: a wonderful place to sit outside on a warm summer's evening, drink a few ales, and watch the tide come and go in the quay.

So eight of us set out on a blustery dry Spring day after meeting at the picnic site opposite Carew Castle. It had been raining all week and, as we knew that we were in for a wet ride, we dressed for the occasion in waterproofs and boots.

After turning left out of the picnic site we rode along the pretty lanes to Carew Newton, chatting and enjoying the day out together. Here the country-side is quite flat and it gave us time to warm up at an easy pace. First a right, and then a left and we were speeding down the hill to Cresswell Quay. At the bottom of the hill on our right was Cresselly Inn. It was open, but as it was so early in the day, we elected to give it a miss this time and call in on our way back. The tide was rising along the estuary, slowly covering the reed beds. The gulls and the pied wagtails bobbed and wove along the waters edge looking for food. Soon we were crossing the old Cresswell Bridge; if you had passed this way a hundred years ago, it would have looked the same as it does today.

After crossing the bridge, we took a right turn onto a bridleway that headed up past Cresswell Farm, and went through a field gate. The bridleway dipped into the valley and started to get very wet and muddy; soon we were crossing one stream after another. Just before the bridleway started to climb, we met the deepest stream of all. Luckily for us, there was a footbridge spanning the deepest part or we would have never made it across. The track started to climb so we slithered our way past Thorn Farm until we reached the main A4075.

At the main road, we turned left and rode along at a fast pace. Although this road is classed as an 'A' road it is never very busy and it is only in the summer months that you see many cars. When we reached Half Way House we turned right through a gate onto another bridleway that ran straight across a field. In the field were two horses, who came to see what we were doing and galloped alongside the bridleway with us. Soon the going became harder as we crossed over marsh land and passed by the site of the old disused Loveston Colliery. Hardly anything can be seen of this once thriving pit, all the buildings have been removed and the only sign left is the track that you cycle on. It was here on May 26th 1936 that Loveston Colliery was the scene of a tragic mine disaster. The water from the old mine workings burst into the main shaft and drowned seven local men. It seems strange as you ride past this peaceful place that men worked and gave their lives to dig coal from the bowels of the earth.

At the houses at Loveston Road we turned left and headed down the hill, but very soon we were climbing up the hill past Loveston School and onto the cross-roads. This road section was very easy, and in no time at all we were turning left into a narrow lane, and on towards the next bridleway. After a few metres of metalled road we passed by Flimstone Farm, turned left on a rough track, and plunged down into a valley. At the bottom of the valley, we crossed a wet section and then climbed to a gate and a bridleway on our right that headed across the fields.

This part was great fun as we rode over the grass and into a wooded section. When we entered the woods we were confronted by a deep stream and a narrow footbridge. John, Ben, Tom and I decided to ride across, though the water was flowing rapidly, and it took all our skill and a bit of luck to get across. The girls decided to ford the stream, first Sheila and Georgina made it across, and then it was Barbara's turn. Barbara was doing well until she reached the middle then her front wheel seemed to sliver in the opposite direction to the way she was going. With one foot caught in the toe clip, Barbara slid sideways into the water. One wet and cold person emerged from the stream to be greeted, I'm ashamed to say, by hysterical laughter from everyone present. It was Jill's turn to cross; she just smiled and crossed over the bridge.

With an assortment of wet items of clothing tied to our bikes we set off through the wood, climbed a bank and rode across another field until we reached Waddock Farm. This old Pembrokeshire farm house was empty and falling into dereliction, and the outbuildings were ready to collapse at any time. A sad forlorn air seemed to radiate from what would have been once a large important farm. We rode by silently, the atmosphere affecting every one.

At the road we turned right and then left, and entered Martlewy, a pretty village with a Post Office and a small picnic site. Today we carried on, because we wanted to be sure to catch the next pub before it closed. The thought of a cool drink spurred us on, so we increased our pace and soon were speeding down the hill on our way to Landshipping and the Stanley Arms. This is a great downhill section, so we made the most of it, trying to milk every metre before we had to pedal again. Soon we were at the Stanley Arms and so we turned into the car park and raced into the pub to get a drink. The Stanley Arms is a quaint little pub situated about one hundred metres from the River Cleddau, today we sat in the garden, devoured packets of crisps and sank a welcome drink.

Refreshed and fed, we turned right out of the pub and headed towards Landshipping Quay. As we rode round the quay, the view across the river was breathtaking; the wind had dropped and the sun was glinting off the water. Across the river, the trees in their Spring finery were a vibrant mixture of pale greens. To make the picture complete, a family of swans with their five little ones spread out behind them came slowly across the quay.

Shortly after the quay the road headed inland, and we cycled on until we reached a wood to our left. Here we turned left onto a narrow path that skirts through the wood, by-passing Woodhouse. We emerged out of the wood by an old iron field gate, passed through onto an old green lane, and cycled across the fields to the road at Broadly Farm. At the road we turned right and went down a pretty little lane that gave tantalising glimpses off the river through the high hedgerow. Slowly we climbed a short hill and sped downwards until we reached a sharp left-hand bend by the remains of St Mary's Church. From here the road climbed again until we reached the cross-roads, where we turned right and descended to Garrons Pill. At the Pill the vista opened out and there was a good view across the river to Benton Wood. We took a deep breath as the road climbed up a steep hill; though only a short climb, it took every ounce of energy to slog our way up. When we reached the top of the hill we heaved a sigh of relief and sped on to Lawrenny.

Lawrenny is a pleasant little village with its old church and small Pembroke-shire cottages. Today the cottages were all freshly painted white after a long wet winter. This is the usual practice in Pembrokeshire; every spring a fresh coat of paint is added to brighten up the place. We rode through the village, passed the cricket ground and took a right fork down a narrow lane. The lane meandered through the almost flat countryside, and we passed by another empty farm at Lawrenny Newton. Farming in this area was once very profitable with early potatoes and rich pasture for milk herds. Nowadays, the farmers are having a rough time with cut backs in the milk quota, cheap early potatoes from the Canary Isles and the dreaded BSE. Bankruptcy is common place in the farming community, and farms that have been owned for generations by one family, are now sadly empty.

At the end of Newton Lane we turned right and pedalled down the hill until we reached Cresswell Bridge. For the second time we crossed over the bridge and cycled on until we came to Cressely Inn. We sat by the quay, the time gently slipping by, chatting and laughing at what we had seen and done on today's ride. With great reluctance we dragged ourselves away from the Inn and started the climb up the hill. As we reached the bend, an elderly man and a woman in motorised wheel chairs came racing down the hill in the opposite direction. "Last one at the pub buys the drinks" was all we could hear them say, as they flashed passed.

We forked right at the top of the hill and descended along a narrow lane until we reached West Williamston. With a slight wiggle in the road we had passed through the village and we were riding along a long flat lane back to Carew. We all became silent, the tiredness from the day's ride keeping us quiet. Very soon we were at the right turning to the picnic site where we had started our journey this morning; we had enjoyed our ride, and it would live in our memories for ever.

Ride 5: Llawhaden Castle, Drim Wood, Wiston, Llawhaden

Abbreviations: O.R.S. Off-road Section; R.S. Road Section.

Distance: 21 miles.

Time: 4 hours.

Terrain: Bridleways and country lanes, 3 steep hills. Moderate.

Map: Ordnance Survey Outdoor Leisure 35 South Pembrokeshire.

This ride passes through some extremely beautiful countryside, mainly along narrow country lanes and bridleways. It passes the ancient castle of Llawhaden and the old hospital, which was once a leper colony. Some tracks are a bit rough and can be very muddy at certain times of the year. The track at the beginning of this ride is very steep and can be very slippy, so take particular care here.

Start: At the car park and picnic site by Llawhaden Castle, grid reference 073 174, which is at the fork of a small lane 200m from the castle.

1. (O.R.S.) Leave the car park with the castle at your back and turn LEFT, then turn immediately LEFT down a narrow lane sign-posted 'No through road'. This is a bridle-path that takes you down a steep hill passing a new bungalow on your right. This old sunken lane is the original entrance to the castle. At the bottom of this rough track you come to a T-junction.

2. (R.S.) At the T-junction turn LEFT. Follow the road with the river on your right. You soon come to the ancient Llawhaden River Bridge to your right; don't cross over the bridge but continue along the road passing the old Llawhaden church on your right. Carry on and climb up a hill with the river still on your right. When the road starts to bend left on your right you will see a Footpath sign into the woods.

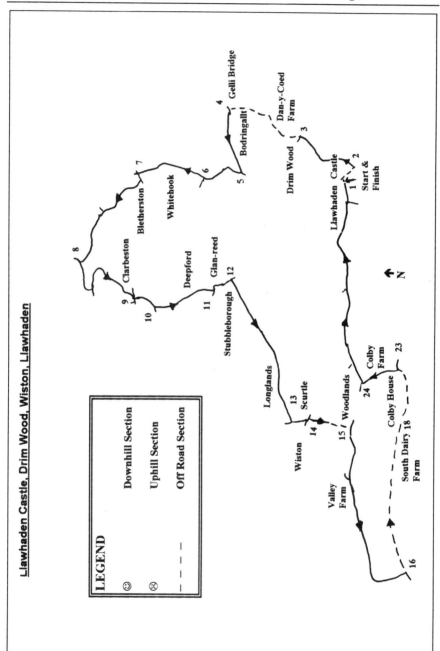

Llawhaden Castle, Drim Wood, Wiston, Llawhaden

LEGEND

☺ Downhill Section

☹ Uphill Section

– – – Off Road Section

3. (O.R.S.) Turn RIGHT into Drim Wood along the bridle-path, grid reference 079 182, and continue down the hill to a gate at Dan-Y-Coed Farm. Go through this gate and pass by the farmhouse, then pass through two more gates next to the cattle sheds. This is the worst part of the ride, for here the cow dung is thick, so don't slip or you won't have anybody near you for the rest of the day. After the farm, ride on along the bridleway keeping the river on your right to the road by Gelli Bridge.

4. (R.S.) At the road turn LEFT and ride on passing a church on your left. Climb up a hill and pass Bodringallt Farm on your left. At the top of the hill you will come to a lane to your right.

5. Turn RIGHT into this lane and go down the steep hill; go around the hairpin bend and pass over the railway bridge. Continue to go down the hill until at the bottom you reach a road to your right.

6. Turn RIGHT and cross over the ford, taking care or you will end up with wet feet. Ride on along this road passing Whitehook Farm on your right to a T-junction.

7. Turn LEFT at this T-junction and you will come to Bletherston old church on your right. There is a lovely picnic site by the village pond and it is well worth stopping for a few minutes to contemplate the rest of your journey. Carry on up the hill and pass through Bletherston at grid reference 070 212. Carry on along this lane ignoring a road to your right and to your left to the T-junction.

8. At the T-junction turn LEFT and ride down the hill and cross over the river bridge. After crossing the bridge, within 30m turn LEFT. Continue along this lane passing a church on your left until you come to the outskirts of Clarbeston.

9. You come to another T-junction, turn RIGHT and enter the village.

10. Pass through the village, ignore the road to your right and then pass by Clarbeston Church on your left and exit the village. Carry on along this road called Deepford Lane, cross over the railway bridge, and ride on to a T-junction.

11. At the T-junction turn LEFT and climb up the steep hill at Glan-reed.

12. At the top of the hill turn RIGHT, pass Stubbleborough Farm on your right and Longlands Farm on your left. Carry on and head towards Wiston to the small cross-roads with Manor Farm ahead of you.

13. Turn LEFT and cycle along this road. Ignore the road forking from your right signposted to Wiston and carry on to a lane to your right, at a place called Scurtle.

14. Turn RIGHT into this lane which is marked as a 'Road used as a Public Footpath' and continue to Woodlands Farm Park and another lane T-junction.

15. When you are at this T-junction turn RIGHT and cycle along this lane. Ignore the road to your right by Valley Farm, ride over Hill Crest; ignore the bridleway to your right to Merryborough Farm, go round the left-hand bend and go down the hill. At the bottom of the hill you will see a road to your left, signposted 'No through road'

16. Turn LEFT into this road. This is an ancient bridleway from South Dairy Mountain to the road at Colby House.

17. (O.R.S.) Keep on the lane along South Dairy Mountain. It soon becomes a rough track and bridleway by a farm, but still keep straight on to another farm to your left called South Dairy Farm.

18. At South Dairy Farm the track bears left into the farm, but you must keep STRAIGHT on and go through an iron field gate and enter the field. Cross the field, following the old bridleway, keeping close to the fence on your right, and head for a field gate in front of you. The track is almost non-existent but you can make out wheel ruts in the ground.

19. When you reach the next field gate, go through it and head STRAIGHT on for a plantation of trees, a field gate and a cottage.

20. Pass through the next gate, and ride past a cottage on your left. Ignore the track that forks to your left, but follow the metalled lane that bears right around the trees. In about 50m you will come to a right-hand bend in the lane; just ahead is Midcounty Farm.

21. At this bend, STRAIGHT ahead of you is a metal field gate; go through this gate and head diagonally across the field to the gate in the far right corner, where you join up with the original bridleway. There is no sign of any track so just head across the open field. The day we came through the gates were difficult to open so we had to carry our bikes over.

22. From this point continue STRAIGHT on across the fields towards Colby House and the field gate in the distance at grid reference 036 162

23. (R.S.) Go through this gate and turn LEFT onto the road. Carry on down the road ignoring the lane to your right and ride on passing Colby Farm on your right.

24. At the right-hand bend, ignore the lane to the left but keep straight on the road ahead. Pass the road to your left, and follow the sign post to Llawhaden. Now keep STRAIGHT on ignoring the two roads to your left to Llawhaden. Grid reference 070 174.

25. Carry on down the hill into Llawhaden, ignoring the road to your right. Soon you will be at the car park where you started your journey, but first take the LEFT fork to the castle up the narrow road, signposted to the castle. Before you end your tour of Llawhaden and Wiston parishes it is well worth the effort to look around the castle and climb the tower for a wonderful view across Slebech Estate and the Preseli Mountains in the distance.

Llawhaden

Llawhaden Castle was built to protect the Bishops of St David's. The castle was built on a high ridge overlooking the Eastern Cleddau. It is difficult to believe that it was built for a serious purpose when you look upon the picturesque beauty of its ruins.

There has been a castle on this site since 1175 but this original castle was razed by the Welsh in 1192. The existing castle was remodelled by Bishop Martyn at the end of the 13th Century and was the stimulus for the development of the adjacent town of Llawhadden. In 1287, Bishop Beck founded a hospital for wayfarers but as this catered for lepers it was situated away from the castle on the outskirts of the village. The remains of the hospital can be seen on your return journey just before you come into Llawhaden.

Llawhaden Castle

Ride 6: St Govan's, Hundleton, Stackpole and Bosherston

Abbreviations: O.R.S. Off-road Section; R.S. Road Section.

Distance: 19 miles.

Time: 4 hours.

Terrain: Bridleways and country lanes, two hills. Easy.

Map: Map Outdoor Leisure 36 South Pembrokeshire.

Start and finish: At the car park at St Govan's. Grid Reference 967 930.

The start of this ride crosses the Castlemartin MOD Danger area which is open to the public only at certain times of the year. This consists of most weekends and Bank holidays, but it is also open at other times as well during the Winter and Summer. To check when the range is open, telephone 01646 661321 extn 4336 and ask (1997) for Major Hancock or telephone the National Park Centre Pembroke 01646 622388. Don't be afraid to cross the firing range when it is open. It is safe, but please keep to the bridleway.

1. (O.R.S.) Leave the car park and then, with the sea facing you, turn RIGHT along the track and head for the gate that takes you along the Pembrokeshire Coast Path and onto the Castlemartin Firing Range. You could visit the little chapel of St Govan's hidden down on the cliff, below. Go through the gate and ride along the coast path to the car park and road at Stack rocks.

(R.S.) Turn RIGHT and ride on the road through the Military Artillery Range to the cross-roads at the B4319.

3. Go STRAIGHT on at the cross-roads. Go down the hill and at the bottom of the hill, at the T-junction turn LEFT.

4. Pass the old cross on your left, and ignore the lane on your left. Ride on through the little village of Warren to a fork in the roads.

5. Fork RIGHT and cycle on to a cross-roads.

6. Go STRAIGHT on at the cross-roads and go down the hill into the valley to a T-junction.

7. Turn RIGHT at the T-junction and pass over Stern bridge and then climb up Axton Hill to the Speculation Inn on your left.

8. (O.R.S.) At the Inn turn RIGHT into a lane marked on the map as a bridleway (not the B4320). Follow the lane passing the lakes on your left and the lake on your right to Orielton Mill on your right.

9. Turn LEFT through a gate and follow a green lane across the fields to a gate and a lane on your right at West Orielton.

10. Turn RIGHT here and go through a gate and ride on to a T-junction.

11. (R.S.) At the T-junction turn LEFT and ride on this lane to a T-junction.

12. Turn RIGHT at this T-junction (this junction is on a sharp bend in the road so you are really going straight on). Cycle on through Maiden Wells, ignore the lanes to your right and left, and ride on to the T-junction at the B4319.

13. Turn RIGHT down the hill and then turn LEFT. Ride on to a road on your left.

14. Go STRAIGHT on, then go round the right-hand bend and descend the hill. Just after you go around another sharp right-hand bend you will come to a fork in the road.

15. Fork LEFT and ride on through the woods and go around another sharp right-hand bend. Continue through the National Trust woodland to a fork in the road.

16. Fork RIGHT and ride on passing Rowston Farm on your left to a cross-roads at Stackpole Elidor.

17. (O.R.S.) Go STRAIGHT on at the cross-roads onto a track that enters the woods. Ride on through the woods following the rough track to a T-junction.

18. (R.S.) At the T-junction turn RIGHT and cycle on to the T-junction At the B4319.

19. When you reach the T-junction turn LEFT and ride on to the staggered cross-roads.

20. At the staggered cross-roads, take the road signposted to Bosherston, which is the second exit on your left.

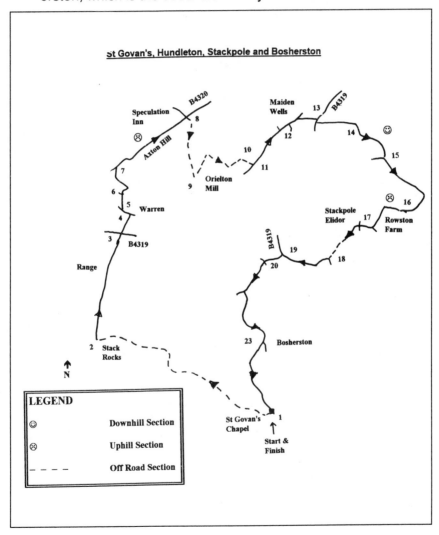

21. Continue on this lane, ignoring the road to your right, to Bosherston.

22. Ride on through the village, pass the tea rooms on your left, and ride on to a fork in the road.

23. Fork RIGHT and follow the sign post to St Govan's Head and Stack Rocks. Continue to follow this road to the car park on your left, where you started your journey.

St Govan's

There are many theories as to the true origin of St Govan's Chapel, most of which are supported more by legend than historical documentation. The most popular belief is that St Govan was Sir Gawain or Gauvaine the Courteous, one of King Arthur knights and nephew, and the slayer of the Green Knight. Others believe that St Govan was Gobhan, the Irish Abbot of Dairinis Monastery. Although it is traditionally reputed to be of Dark Age origin the existing building only dates back to the 13th Century, although the altar and bench probably date from the 5th Century. There is a little well near the entrance that is supposed to have healing properties for those suffering from diseases of the eyes, and another well lies below the chapel which was said to cure lameness. The pilgrims who were cured left their crutches behind as proof to the effectiveness of the well. I must wonder however, how a genuinely crippled person would have made it down those slippery steps to the well! The well is dry, so I suppose we will never know if it worked.

Flimston Chapel

This sad, deserted 15th Century chapel is only accessible when the range is not in use. It is a similar chapel to St Govan's but is larger and much restored. It is one of the many buildings which form the ghost town left behind when the land was taken over by the Military. Nearby is ruined Flimston Farm which was Medieval in origin with later additions in the 18th or 19th Centuries.

The Castlemartin Range

More than 6000 acres of land in the National Park are held by the Military. These include the spectacular cliffs between St Govan's and Stack Rocks. Many people are opposed to the military having a presence in the National Park and causing limited access to this wonderful coastline. It is, however, the largest area of unimproved grassland in Wales, and so provides an important and safe habitat for many birds to breed, in an area untouched by insecticides – though they must keep a look out for the occasional shell!

Bosherton Lily Ponds

The lily ponds at Bosherton were artificially created on limestone in the late 18th century and early 19th century by the Stackpole Estate. They are important havens for waterfowl and waders.

May and June are a wonderful time to visit them as they are resplendent with the beautiful white bowls of the lilies soaking up the summer sun. Bright blue dragonflies hover above them, and the tracks are bordered on all sides by an assortment of wild flowers such as the scarlet pimpernel, speedwell, irises and orchids. As you follow the lily ponds to where they join the beach, you come to a small stream which runs into the sea. One day while we were walking alongside this stream we saw a writhing black mass. On investigation it turned out to be thousands of elvers struggling upstream to reach the lily ponds at the end of their long journey from the Sargasso Sea. Life is hard, however, for no sooner did they reach the pond than an elderly eel was awaiting them with his mouth open, and many of them soon became his dinner. The lucky ones escaped this cannibal, but still more of them were eaten by the birds. It's amazing really that any of them survive to become adult eels.

If you walk around these ponds early in May, take care where you are treading because often we have chanced upon adders warming themselves in the sun. They have just awakened from hibernation and so are very slow to move. Later in the year they will quickly slither away when they hear you approach. If you do come across one, just leave it alone and pass carefully by. They are more afraid of you than you are of them.

The beach here is absolutely fantastic with golden sands which never seem to be crowded. There are many rock pools, some of which are quite deep and ideal for young children to bathe in. The rolling dunes are scattered with many beautiful wild flowers such as sea holly and burnet rose. This is one of our favourite spots and it is well worth coming back another day to walk around.

How was it for us?

The mist rising from the water,
Cast a shroud upon the rock.
The sea was white and tormented,
The ground rumbled to the shock.
And the ancient bell of St Govan's
Chimed softly in the air.
While sea nymphs dance around the magic well,
Every sailor must take care.

D. Thomas Palmer

St Govan's Chapel must be one of the most wonderful places to visit in the British Isles. This tiny chapel set at the bottom of a steep cliff conjures up for anyone visiting it, all the magic and mystery that surrounds this part of Pembrokeshire. There are legends of Knights, Merlin the magician, and King Arthur and the round table. Every county in England and Wales may lay claim to being the site of King Arthur's Camelot, but this tiny chapel on the cliff most closely fits the description of Sir Gauvaine's resting place after his battle with the Green Knight. Sir Gauvaine, one of King Arthur's Knights and nephew, hid from his enemies in a cleft in the rock. When recovered from his wounds, he did penance in a little church set in the rocks overlooking the sea. Folklore maintains that this is the place.

So, on a bright and cold Sunday morning in January, the six of us decided to head off and complete the St Govan's circular bike route. We parked in the car park not far from the cliff edge; leaving our bikes fastened to the cars, we decided to walk down the coast path and visit St Govan's Chapel, which was way below us at the foot of the cliff. Today a strong east wind was blowing and the surf was pounding on the rocks below us. Large wisps of milky white foam came blowing and tumbling up the cliff face to splatter into huge wet patches on our clothes. A flight of wet slippery limestone steps wound down to the chapel, and legend has it that 'no mortal can count them the same up and down'. Today we decided to put this legend to the test, but as we are just mere mortals, every one of us came up with a different count.

After visiting the chapel we walked the short path back to the cars and set off on our bikes. We passed through the gate that leads onto the firing range and cycled along a wide stony track running parallel to the sea. On our right the flat pasture land of Stackpole and Newtown Down spread out before us, not used or changed for years since the army took it over for a training area. To our left was a coast line of towering cliffs broken up with curious fissures, funnels, caldrons and precipices that plunged down to the foaming sea. Not a place to stray near the edge! Soon, on our left, we came to Huntsman's Leap – one of the most striking of these cliff fissures; it gets its name 'from a legend that a Huntsman riding his horse at full gallop didn't see it until it was too late and had no option but to leap across this terrifying chasm. We stood near the edge and looked down into the fissure, the sea was a boiling ferment as it crashed in and out. A long discussion was started on whether it would be possible to leap across on a horse, a mountain bike, or indeed on foot. The conclusion was you would have to be crazy to try, or that you wished to die prematurely.

Relieved to be away from the edge of the chasm, we cycled on along the track that wound its way alongside the cliff top, about ten metres from the edge. The views in each direction were simply stunning and as we rode further west so the cliffs, with names like The Castle, Mewsford Point, Bullslaughter Bay and Flimstone Point, climbed higher and higher. Blow holes litter the cliff top and occasionally the sea rushing into them causes a reverberation that sounds like a cannon, that echoes around the countryside. Sometimes spray is shot high into the air from these holes, and the sunlight passing through the water vapour creates miniature rainbows. The most spectacular view was saved until the last

Huntsman's Leap

at Stack Rocks: these shear cliffs soar out of the sea, framed with the Green Bridge as a back drop.

At the car park we turned right and rode inland on a lane across Flimstone Down. To our right and left we passed little villages, long deserted because of the armies need to requisition the surrounding countryside. Sad and forlorn is the only way to describe these abandoned houses, farms and churches. The army provides money so that each year the local people can come back to try to maintain the buildings in their original condition but no matter how hard they try, emptiness and loneliness still prevail.

When we reached the cross-roads with the B4319 we headed straight across and descended the hill. Here the countryside was lush and green in contrast to Flimstone Down due to the use of nitrate fertilisers on the fields. Before very long we reached the bottom of the hill and climbed up to the T-junction, then we turned left and rode through the little village of Warren. After passing through the village we forked right and at the cross-roads we went straight on. First the road was flat then it plummeted into the valley, to reach a T-junction at Stern Bridge. Turning right, we started to climb up Axton Hill, which was the first really hard climb on the ride. Puffing and panting round the first bend we all thought that we had reached the top, but no such luck. The road flattened out and then went even steeper until it levelled out just before the Speculation Inn. This was a slog of a hill and we were all glad to reach the top.

Until now the morning had been cold but sunny with an east wind off the sea, but here higher and away from the sea, the temperature had dropped considerably. Frost gave the trees and hedges a coat of white, and icicles hung from fences like glass chandeliers. To our left the Salutation Inn was open, so we decided that now was the time to stop and have a quick drink, a packet of crisps and a warm in front of the log fire.

After the warmth of the Inn the cold bit at our faces as we turned right down the bridleway that led to Orielton Mill. Soon the bridleway became a rough flat shale track that weaved its way past some woods and two large frozen ponds to the left and the right. Wild fowl mustered like cold men on parade around a small hole in the ice, each taking its turn to wet its feet and beak. Cycling on until we reached the old mill, we turned left through an iron field gate and followed a green track across the fields in a northerly direction. Today with the ground frozen hard we did not have the usual problem of mud, but instead the tracks were bumpy and rutted which made steering extremely difficult at times. At the end of the green track we turned right through a gate and entered a narrow bridleway that led us past Orielton Wood. We continued onto the road at East Orielton.

Relieved to be at the road after the hard bumpy bridleway we turned left and followed the lane through Maiden Wells, until we reached the B4319 Pembroke road. Turning quickly right and then left we cycled along a flat lane across the top of Myrtle Hill. On our left, way below in the valley, lay Pembroke Town with the flag on top of the castle keep waving in the stiff breeze. Anyone visiting

Pembroke from this direction five hundred years ago would have been in awe at the size and majesty of the castle that lay before them. After turning a sharp right-hand bend, the lane suddenly plummeted down a steep hill. With tall hedges flashing past on both sides we raced to the bottom of the hill and the wood at Trustle Mill. Soon at a small wood aptly named Bottoms we forked right and rode on down a flat lane through a pretty valley of rich pasture and coppices before reaching a sharp right-hand bend.

Here we turned the bend and entered a beautiful wood of coniferous and deciduous trees owned by the National Trust. Even on a cold winter day the wood was a blaze of colour. The last of the copper coloured leaves littered the woodland floor, broken by the dark green of Holly and the purple tinged green of the tall Spruce. Birds winged back and forth among the branches and the warning cries of the robin rang out as we cycled past. A pair of squirrels chased each other playfully through the upper canopy leaping from branch to branch, better than any acrobat at the circus. Eventually we took a right fork in the roads and started to climb up a hill out of the wood. Slowly we all toiled up the hill and at a sharp left-hand bend the road flattened out. Riding through open winter fields we reached and passed through the farm buildings of Rowston Farm and then cycled to the cross-roads at Stackpole Elidor.

The old church of Stackpole Elidor stood on our right, stark against the leafless winter trees. We went straight over the cross-roads and rode down a track that passed through the woods at Cheriton Bottom. This narrow rough track wound its way through the woods, crossed over two small wooden bridges, and descended slowly until it reached the road. We turned right and cycled along a quiet lane through a pleasant valley. This area of woodland, owned by the Natural Trust, was once the grounds of Stackpole Court, which used to stand to the left of the road. At the first small turning on our left, that led to the Court, we stopped and rode the few metres to the old bridge which spans the man-made lakes. These lakes run in a southerly direction almost down to the sea and in season they are covered in beautiful flowering water lilies. There is a path that runs around this Nature Reserve and it is well worth the effort to return on another day and walk the path from the bridge to the sea at Broad Haven.

It was late in the afternoon and the last of the winter sun was beginning to fade fast, so we left the old bridge and rode down the lane until we reached the road at the B4319. Here we turned left and at the next cross-roads we turned left again and cycled on to Bosherston. Usually we would have stopped in the village and had a cup of tea at the tea rooms but today as darkness was drawing on we kept straight on. After the village we took the right fork to St Govan's and cycled with increased speed to dodge the impending gloom. Within five minutes we had reached the car park on our left where we had started our journey. We were cold, tired and very hungry but it had been a wonderful ride around this magical area.

Ride 7: Johnston, and the Old Great Western Railway

Abbreviations: O.R.S. Off-road Section; R.S. Road Section.

Distance: 18 miles.

Time: 3 hours.

Terrain: Country lanes and bridleways.

Map: Ordnance Survey Outdoor Leisure, South Pembrokeshire.

This is one of the easiest rides in the book, suitable for anyone wishing to take a child in a rear baby seat. It is mainly along well surfaced bridleways and cyclepaths on the old disused Great Western Railway.

Start and finish: Near Johnston Railway Station. Grid reference 932 107

Do be very careful, when descending the very steep slope from the bridge. We did also find that some of the cycle stiles were very low, so please mind your child's head.

The route passes near to Westfield Pill Nature Reserve which is managed by Dyfed Wildlife Trust. You may wish to lock up your bikes and make a small detour to visit this interesting wildlife habitat.

For those of you who are interested in boats this route passes alongside Neyland Marina. You may wish to stop here, admire the magnificent boats moored here and dream of how you would spend your lottery winnings! On a more mundane level, this is an excellent place to have a cup of tea.

1. Park near the railway station, leave the car park and turn RIGHT onto the main Haverfordwest to Milford Haven road.

2. Proceed along the main road and take the second turning on your LEFT just past the old church.

3. Go down the hill and take the first turning LEFT to Rosemarket. Cross over the railway bridge and go down the hill towards Rosemarket. Just before Rosemarket, climb the short hill and enter the village. Ride on, ignoring the turning to your left and go STRAIGHT on over the staggered cross-roads. Carry on, ignore the turning to your left, and ride out of the village to a fork in the road. **From here, you can start to follow the Blue and White Cycle Way mark signs**

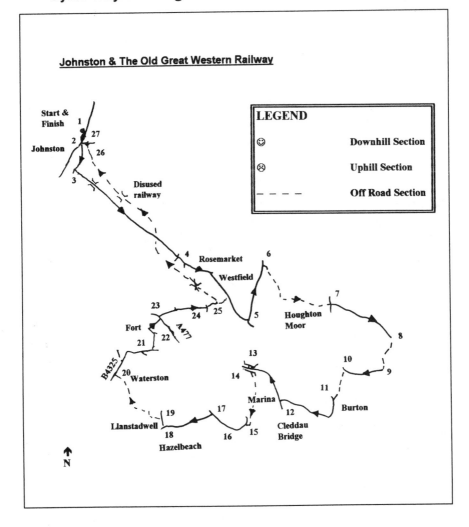

4. At the fork turn LEFT and go down the hill passing Westfield Hill farm to a T-junction.

5. Turn LEFT at the T-junction and climb up the hill to the bridleway on your right sign-posted with the blue and white sign.

6. Turn RIGHT onto the bridleway and cycle on across Houghton Moor to the road at Houghton village.

7. Go STRAIGHT on at the cross-roads and proceed to a bridleway forking off to your right.

8. Fork RIGHT and ride on passing Mountains Park Farm to a road.

9. Turn RIGHT onto the road and ride on until your reach another bridleway on your left.

10. Turn LEFT onto the bridleway and cycle on into Burton passing the church on your left. Pass through the village to the T-junction.

11. At the T-junction turn LEFT and go down the hill. Ignore the turning on your left to Burton Ferry and the pub and climb the hill to the main road by the Cleddau Bridge.

12. When you reach the main road turn RIGHT and ride on until you cross over the next river bridge. At the far side of the bridge look out for the Cycle Path sign on your right.

13. Here turn RIGHT and go down a very steep track – don't try to ride down this slope as it is quite dangerous.

14. At the bottom of the slope turn RIGHT and with the river on your left ride along the old track of the Great Western Railway to the Marina at Brunel Quay. It is well worth stopping here at the café to rest and watch the world go by before carrying on with your journey.

15. Ride along the road to the T-junction where you turn LEFT onto the B4325

16. Cycle along the B4325 with the Daugleddau River Estuary on your left to the first turning on your left to Hazelbeach.

17. Turn LEFT here and ride through Llanstadwell, passing the old church on your left. Carry on to the first turning to your right.

18. Turn RIGHT up the hill, ignore the first turning on your left into a new estate and just past the estate look out for the blue and white way mark on your left.

19. Turn LEFT onto a bridleway and climb up, passing Hazel Hill House, to the T-junction at Waterston.

20. Turn RIGHT at the T-junction onto the B4325. Ride on along the B road, ignore the first road on your left and go round the right-hand bend. Here shrouded in trees on your left is the disused Scoveston Fort. Ride on for just a few yards to the next turning on your left.

21. Turn LEFT here, and within 100m turn LEFT again. Ride on to a T-junction.

22. At the T-junction turn LEFT, ride on down the lane, go round a sharp right-hand bend and ride on to the main A477 road.

23. Turn LEFT at the main road, go down the hill and within a short distance turn RIGHT.

24. Cycle on down this lane to a T-junction where you turn RIGHT. You then turn LEFT and go down a hill. to the entrance on your left to the path of the disused Great Western Railway which is now used as a cycle path.

25. Here you turn LEFT under the cycle stile and continue on the cycle path to the town at Johnston. On the way you pass over two road junctions. **Ignore the blue and white cycle way signs.** When you are nearly at Johnston, the cycle path narrows and crosses over two stiles and runs beside the present-day railway until it reaches a T-junction at the council estate in Johnston.

26. Turn LEFT at the T-junction go through the estate to another T-junction where you turn LEFT again.

27. Ride on to the main A4076 Haverfordwest road where you turn RIGHT. Very soon you will reach the turning on your LEFT into the railway station where you started your journey.

Ride 8: Dale, Marloes, St Brides Haven, St Ishmaels, Dale

Abbreviations: O.R.S. Off-road Section; R.S. Road Section.

Distance: 18 miles.

Time: 3 hours.

Terrain: Lanes and bridleways. Easy.

Map: Ordnance Survey Outdoor Leisure 36, South Pembrokeshire.

Start and finish: At the car park just north of Dale. Grid Reference 809 067.

---

1. (R.S.) With the sea at your back turn RIGHT out of the car park and proceed along the coast road towards Haverfordwest. Ignore the first turning on your left and the track to your left, cross over the bridge and cycle on to the first road on your left signposted to Marloes.

2. Turn LEFT and ride up the hill to a fork in the roads.

3. Fork LEFT, enter Marloes and go past an estate of houses on your left.

4. After the houses take the first on your LEFT by the church. Cycle along this lane passing Marloes Court on your left to a fork in the road. To visit Marloes Sands then, just after Marloes Court, turn left onto a bridleway that takes you down to the beach. After swimming or just sun bathing, return to the road, turn left and carry on with your journey.

5. (O.R.S.) Turn RIGHT at the fork and ride through the car park. At the far end of the car park you will come to a track which is a 'Road used as a Footpath'; follow this to a T-junction.

6. (R.S.) At the T-junction turn LEFT and cycle on to the car park at Martins Haven Point. This is a good point to leave your bikes

locked to the fence and walk up to Jack Sound and look out over Skomer and Skokholm Islands.

7. After looking around the point return the way you came, ignoring the track you came on to your right. Cycle on towards Marloes. Just as you enter the village you will pass the 30mph signs; ride on for about 50m until you see another 30mph sign on a lamp post opposite Caprice House. Fork LEFT on to a bridleway.

8. (O.R.S.) Follow the bridleway to Winterton Farm. The bridleway turns LEFT through an iron field gate into an open field. Follow

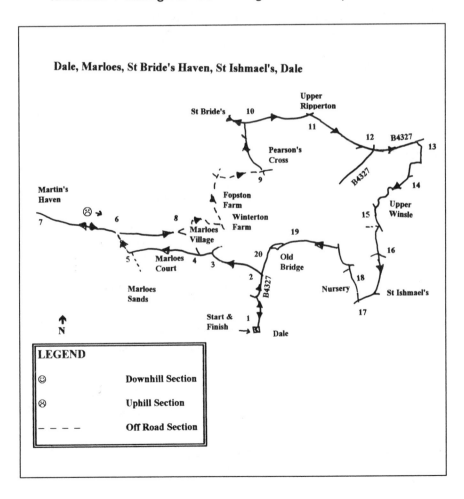

the bridleway across the open field to another field gate, go through the gate and cross the next field to a gate at Fopston Farm. Pass through the gate and farm and head along the metalled road ignoring the track to your right. Go down the hill, pass through the wood and climb the hill to the cross-roads at Pearsons Cross, with the houses at Kensington Place on your left.

9.   (R.S.) At the cross-roads turn LEFT and cycle on to the road to your left sign-posted to St Brides.

10.   Turn LEFT and cycle into St Brides Bay. After visiting St Brides Haven retrace your path back up the hill ignore the road you came down, and carry on to the right-hand bend at Upper Ripperton Farm.

11.   Ignore the two tracks to your left and keep on around the right-hand bend. Follow the lane, ignoring the road on your right to the cross-roads with the B4327.

12.   Go STRAIGHT on at the cross-roads along the B4327 to the first road on your right.

13.   Turn RIGHT and carry on along this lane to a fork in the roads.

14.   Fork RIGHT, signposted to Upper Winsel Farm, and go down into the valley passing Upper Winsel on your left. Carry on to a T-junction.

15.   Turn LEFT at the T-junction, head up the hill, ignore the tracks to your right and left to a cross-roads.

16.   At the cross-roads, go STRAIGHT on and cycle on down to St Ishmaels. Go through the village, pass the Post Office on your right and ride on to the cross-roads.

17.   Turn RIGHT up the hill and leave St Ishmaels village. Carry on this lane, ignoring the lane to your left. Go round the right-hand bend and climb the hill, passing the Garden Nursery on your left.

18.   Go on past the nursery ignoring the road on your left and the two roads to your right, to a T-junction at the B4327.

19. Turn LEFT at the T-junction on the B4327, ride down the hill and, just for fun, go over the old bridge.

20. Keep on the B4327, ignoring all roads to your right, to the car park in Dale on your LEFT, where you started your journey.

St Brides Haven

St Brides Haven is a pretty little bay, overlooked by its austere Medieval church and by the mock-gothic residence of St Brides 'Castle'. If you walk down the wooded drive to the castle, on either side of the road you will see the ruined walls and buildings of St Brides Abbey which is believed to date from the late Middle Ages.

The chapel of St Bride, which stood on the headland north of the church, has already been claimed by the wild seas around the bay. It is believed that this building marked the site of the original Dark Age Site, because coastal erosion has uncovered earlier Christian type coffins of between 900 and 1500 years old, which can be seen protruding from the cliffs.

Looking across to Skomer Island, Dale Peninsula

How was it for us?

As a boy, I often came on holiday with my parents to this area. The most wonderful part of being on holiday was playing on the beach, building sand castles that would hold off the encroaching tide for ever, and eating gritty sandwiches in the shade of the windbreak. I always thought, until I was twelve, that sandwiches were so named because they were always full of sand! My favourite fillings were banana and Bovril, not together but eaten in separate mouthfuls until I felt full. You see I could do these outrageous things when I was on holiday.

The coast line of Pembrokeshire is without doubt its crowning glory, its pièce de resistance, so to come to this area and not visit the coast would be a crime. Today pack your bucket and spade, tie your towel to the crossbar and if the sun is shining put your sun cream in the saddlebag, for this ride visits two wonderful beaches where you can swim and get a tan.

On a warm Sunday in June the six of us – Barbara, John, Jill, Tom, Ben and myself – set off from the car park on the outskirts of Dale and rode north along the coast road. It was a beautiful day, one of those days when you can't distinguish where the blue of the sea meets the blue of the sky. Out in the bay, yachts in full sail slowly tacked back and forth trying to capture every bit of the sparse breeze. We cycled along the flat road, crossed over a bridge and we turned left up a hill towards Marloes. On our left we passed by some old disused buildings left over from the second world war, falling into disrepair and dereliction, with the odd building housing cattle and sheep. Today you would never believe that this was once an airfield where Spitfires roared out day and night to protect the towns of Milford Haven and Pembroke Dock from the German bombers.

At the top of the hill the road flattened out and we forked left and entered Marloes. On our left was a row of council houses, all now owned by their occupants, as the usual uniformity had disappeared. There were doors of all styles and colours and the gardens were a riot of colour. After the houses we turned left, entered a narrow lane and cycled on until we reached Marloes Court. Just after the Court we decided to make a detour, so we turned left down a bridleway that lead to Marloes Sands.

Marloes Sands, one of the most beautiful beaches in Pembrokeshire, has escaped the ravages of commercialism thanks to the ten-minute walk along the bridleway. Not that we found it very far to ride along this path on our bikes, but it is far enough to deter the ice-cream vans and all the other tourist essentials. There is nothing here but rock pools, hidden caves and the waves lapping on a golden beach overlooked only by the uninhabited Gateholm Island. We arrived with the tide halfway up the beach which would give us at least an hour before the sea would completely cover this wonderful cove. After scrambling down the path onto the beach we stripped off our clothes and sat soaking up the sun. Even though it was the weekend and the weather was so good there was only a smattering of people on the sands.

About 50m to our right two very large ladies were helping their offspring, two girls and a boy of about seven, to change into their swimsuits. This was aided by a huge changing tent that the children disappeared into with either one or both of their mothers. It was like watching a pantomime show as first one large lady vanished head first under this voluminous garment, with one or both large posteriors poking out into the sunshine. Reluctantly after about half an hour relaxing on the beach we decided it was time to press on with our journey; we emptied the sand out of our shoes and headed back up the bridleway to the road.

Turning left onto the road, we rode on until we reached a car park. We cycled through to the rear of the car-park and emerged onto a rough bridleway that led to a T-junction. We turned left onto a lane that passed through a wonderful patchwork of golden fields bordered on both sides by the sea. With ever-increasing speed we cycled down the hill towards the car park at Martins Haven. We locked our bikes to a wooden fence and walked across the headland to look out over Jack Sound at the islands of Skomer and Skokholm, shimmering in the summer's heat. Both these Islands are uninhabited except for the occasional warden watching over the thousands of birds that use these rugged islands to breed.

Retracing our steps to our bikes, we returned up the hill. It was so easy coming down but we realised just how steep the hill really was, as we climbed breathlessly back to the top. At the outskirts of Marloes, we turned left, just past the 30mph speed limit sign, and entered into a rough bridleway. This old green lane rough, narrow and overgrown in places crossed over the fields until Winterton Farm. Here we turned left through an iron field gate and headed straight across a wide open field to a gate at Fopstone Farm. As we passed through the gate an old sheep dog came barking to greet us, tail wagging, backed up by two large tabby cats who were not going to let us pass until we had given them some fuss. The barking attracted the attention of the farmer who came out to see why his dog was making such a noise. Seeing us with our bikes he exclaimed "You have picked a wonderful day for a bike ride, I wish I could join you!" Pleasantries over, we cycled along a narrow lane that skirted the edge of a wood until we reached a cross-roads at Pearson Cross. We turned left and rode on to turn left again at St Brides Cross and head down the hill into the peaceful cove of St Brides Haven.

St Brides Haven is a lovely place, it has a horseshoe of low cliffs sheltering a sandy cove with brightly painted cottages scattered to the right. Set on a buff to the left is the austere medieval church and in the background sheltering in a grove of trees stands the mock-gothic St Brides Castle. The original chapel of St Brides which once stood near to the church has long been swept away by the savage westerly gales that often roar in from the Atlantic during the winter months. Today, all that can be seen of this once-important chapel are the exposed graves that emerge out of the cliff face like some Transylvanian nightmare. Nearing midday we decided that this was the ideal place to stop for lunch. Sitting on a grassy bank overlooking the cove, we ate a meal of salted crisps and ham sandwiches, washed down with orange squash. In the cove, a group of divers was exploring the rocky depths, their black wet-suit covered heads rising and falling in the water like ducks fishing in a pond. The sun was warm, yet a soft breeze blowing in off the sea kept us contented as we lay, sprawled out like beached whales on the grassy knoll. An hour slipped by before we dragged ourselves away from this peaceful spot and with reluctance began to cycle back up the hill away from St Brides Haven.

The road out of St Brides slowly climbed until we reached Upper Riperton Farm, then it levelled out and we cycled across a flat plain, the view obstructed on both sides of the lane by high overgrown hedgerows. At the cross-roads we rode straight on and took two right turns. On either side of the road were fields of ripening corn and maize swaying in the gentle breeze. Large black crows sat bobbing on the telephone wires that followed the road, waiting their turn to have a dinner of the farmer's crops. Suddenly only ten metres in front of us, a large dog fox with his bushy tail streaming out behind, crossed the road from right to left and disappeared as quickly as he had arrived into the enveloping hedge. No doubt he was as surprised to see us as we were to see him.

After we passed Upper Winsel Farm the road descended into the valley. We crossed over a little bridge and climbed a steep narrow hill until we came to a cross-roads. Following the signpost to St Ishmaels we quickly arrived in the little village; not what you would call pretty, but it does have a certain charm of its own. We turned right out of the village and climbed a hill that led to the junction with the B4327 road. Here we turned left and rode down a steep hill and crossed over Mullock Bridge. Road improvements have left the old Mullock Bridge standing forlorn and unused except for the occasional walker, but we decided to give this ancient bridge six more passengers as we detoured across its narrow parapets on the way to Dale.

Soon we were back on the coast road that we had ridden on earlier in the day. In its switch back way the road continued until we reached the car-park where we had started our journey. We were dusty and tired but it had been a pleasant and enjoyable day along the Marloes Peninsular.

Ride 9: Roch Castle, Nolton Haven, Simpson Cross, Plumstone Mountain

Abbreviations: O.R.S. Off-road Section; R.S. Road Section.

Distance: 21 miles.

Time: 4 hours.

Terrain: Country lanes and bridleways; two hard climbs and one rough stretch. Medium to Hard, depending on time of the year.

Map: North and South Pembrokeshire Outdoor Leisure 35 & 36.

Start and finish: At the lay-by on the A487 St David's to Haverfordwest road, grid reference 876 208. 100m south of Roch cross-roads, almost opposite the Roch Gate Motel.

This ride takes you around the pleasant area of Roch Parish on quite country lanes and bridleways. You visit the pretty harbour of Nolton Haven, the ancient church of Camrose, cross the wilds of Plumstone mountain and call at the wonderful Roch Castle.

1. Turn RIGHT out of the lay-by onto the A487 and cycle to the Roch cross-roads, just a short distance away.

2. At the cross-roads turn LEFT and go down the hill. Follow this lane passing Bathesland Farm and Trefrane Farm and climb to the T-junction.

3. When you reach the T-junction turn LEFT, climb a slight hill and go down the hill to Nolton Haven with the beach and the sea on your right. Cycle through Nolton Haven, ignoring the road to your left, then carry on to a slight fork in the roads.

4. Take the LEFT fork and ride along the valley with the river on your left, not that you can see much of the river, to Nolton; ignore the road to your right.

5. Cycle through the village and pass the Parish Church and Nolton Crest on your left. Carry on to the cross-roads at Nolton Cross.

6. Turn LEFT, and start the long slow climb, ignoring the No Through Road to your left and carry on to the cross-roads at the A487 by Simpson Cross.

7. When you reach the cross-roads go STRAIGHT across and take the first turning RIGHT into a housing estate. Ignore the roads to your right and left but when you reach a T-junction almost back at the main A487 turn LEFT – this avoids riding along the main road. On your right you will see an entrance to the Victorian Tea Rooms where you can have a cup of tea and cake(s).

8. After you have gorged yourself on cake, continue up the hill away from the main road to a fork in the roads. Fork RIGHT and carry on to a T-junction. Turn LEFT and enter Keeston. Fork LEFT again, and pass a church on your left and ignore the road to your right. Follow this road to the next turning right.

9. Take the RIGHT turning signposted to Dudwell and cycle along this lane to a cross-roads in Camrose by the old Parish Church.

10. At the cross-roads turn LEFT, and ride out of the village to a five-way cross-roads.

11. Turn LEFT at the five ways and cycle on passing Robleston Hall and Causeway Farm on your left. After Causeway Farm, carry on to the woodland on your right. Cycle on for a few metres until the road turns sharp left and there is a bridleway into the woods to your right.

12. (O.R.S.) Turn RIGHT on to the bridleway and ride on through the woods to a small factory to your left. Fork RIGHT and ride on a track across an open field and onto the open moor land of Plumstone Mountain. Straight ahead you can see the tumuli on top of Plumstone Mountain. Soon you will reach a fork in the tracks, fork RIGHT and follow the blue way marks along a narrow track that follows the edge of the field boundaries. Pass through a gate and enter a narrow unsurfaced lane and cycle on to the T-junction.

13. (O.R.) When you reach the T-junction at the B4330 turn LEFT. Ignore the lane to your right and cycle on to a narrow metalled track on your left, just a short distance away. This track is marked as a bridleway on the map.

14. (O.R.S.) At the track turn LEFT and follow the bridleway up the

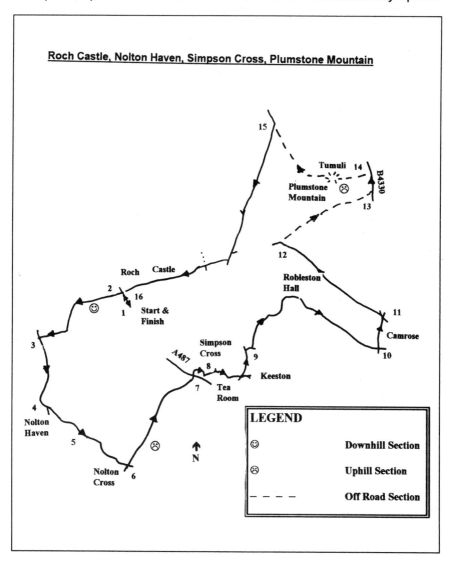

hill to the top of Plumstone Mountain. Cross over a cattle grid and pass the reservoir on your right. When you reach the top pass Plumstone rock and tumuli on your left. This is a good place to stop and have a picnic and look out over the whole of North Pembrokeshire. Ride on the rough track to a gate, go through the gate and head STRAIGHT on across the field heading to the RIGHT of a small mound where you will find a stile. Up to this point there are blue way marks but, from now on, these cease to exist and the going gets a bit tougher. Go over the stile, turn LEFT and follow the fence around the field to on your left an over-grown entrance into a sunken old lane. Pass down into the sunken lane with barbed wire fences on both sides. Push or ride your bike along the narrow and over-grown path, don't turn back – you *can* get through! We came through in late August when the bracken and brambles were at their worst and though it was a struggle, we made it. Soon the path gets less overgrown and starts to meander alongside the field hedges, but keep heading in a north-westerly direction and you soon come to a wide track. Follow this track to the T-junction.

15. (R.S.) At the T-junction turn LEFT and cycle along this road. Climb the hill and ignore the roads to your right; continue and ignore the road to your left by Corner House. Take the next RIGHT fork, ignore the road to your left and head on towards Roch Castle, ahead of you on top of the hill. Climb the hill and pass the Castle on your right. Carry on through the village to the cross-roads at the main A487 road.

16. This is where you turn LEFT and then turn LEFT again into the lay-by where you started your journey.

Nolton Church and Nolton Haven

The pretty village and harbour of Nolton Haven, set in a peaceful sheltered bay is a wonderful place to spend a few hours during the summer months. Today you would not realise its recent past as a port that exported locally-mined anthracite coal. On the cliff side levels are the remnants of the Tudor coal workings where once local men, women and children worked in terrible conditions to make a meagre living.

Nolton Church and the nearby rectory were both built in the Middle Ages. The church contains an impressive, though damaged, stone effigy of an armoured knight, which was used until recently as a gatepost at a local farm.

Camrose

This Medieval settlement, with its castle and church, lies in a wooded valley. The castle has unfortunately been split into two by

Roch Castle

the road to Keeston, the bailey on one side and the 25 ft high motte on the other. The motte is hidden in a clump of rhododendrons and is now part of an ornamental garden. The 14th century parish church has some modernisation but is still an attractive building. It has a cushion font of 12th century date and a nave of an earlier Norman church.

Roch Castle

The castle was built by Adam de Rupe around 1200 on a lofty chunk of volcanic rock. Legend has it that the Lord of the Castle was told by a soothsayer that he would die by the bite of a local adder; he walled himself inside the castle, never leaving for years, but this was of no avail. On the night of his demise, the snake was brought inadvertently into the castle in a basket of firewood. While putting a log onto the fire, the unsuspecting De Rupe was bitten by the snake and the Lord of the Castle died the next day. All that remains of the earlier fortress is a small earthwork bailey at the foot of the rock and the tower dating about 1300 with 15th century additions. During the Civil War the castle was held by Royalists, and during the siege by Oliver Cromwell, the Royalist commander saw Cromwell on his horse close to the castle. The commander, hoping to kill such an important leader, launched a javelin at him. This cut through the strap of Cromwell's helmet and almost cut short the famous man's career. You can stay as a guest at the castle as there is a self contained holiday flat there. What a pleasant place for a holiday – as long as you watch out for the snakes!

Ride 10: St David's Cathedral and St David's Peninsula

Abbreviations: O.R.S. Off-road Section; R.S. Road Section.

Distance: 18 miles.

Time: 3-4 hours.

Terrain: Lanes and bridleways. Only one hard climb. Easy.

Map: Outdoor Leisure 35 North Pembrokeshire.

Start and finish: At car park, ½ mile outside St David's on main A487 near Marine Life Centre. Grid Reference 756 252.

---

1. (O.R.S) Leave the car park at the rear entrance and turn LEFT out of the car park, onto the road to Caerfi Bay. Turn RIGHT at the cross-roads, shown as a fork in the road on the Ordnance Survey map, but the road to the left has been built since the map was printed. Pass a new housing estate on your right. At the last of the new houses turn RIGHT and fork LEFT onto a gravelled bridleway. Keep on the gravelled path, ignoring a road to your right and continue to a lane. On your left you will see the Warpool Court Hotel. You can make a detour left here to visit St Nons.

2. (R.S.) At the lane turn RIGHT down a hill.

3. Almost at the bottom of the hill ignore the narrow road to your left, and cycle on to a T-junction where you turn RIGHT. This road heads up the hill into St David's.

4. When you reach the town square turn LEFT and turn immediately LEFT again; go down the hill passing under the Cathedral Gate. Go down the hill with the Cathedral on your right.

5. Soon take the RIGHT fork and either pass over the bridge or ride through the ford. Pass the old Bishops Palace on your left and carry STRAIGHT on ignoring the metalled road to your right.

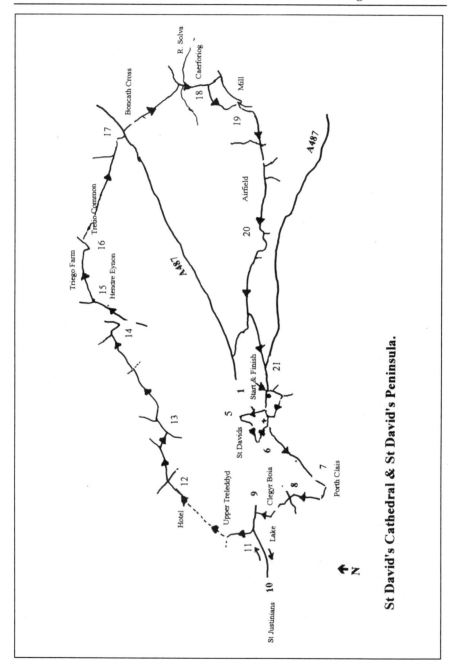

St David's Cathedral & St David's Peninsula.

Start to climb the hill on a rough track and take the LEFT fork. At the top of the hill turn LEFT at the T-junction.

6. Continue along this road and take the first turning on your LEFT and ride down the hill. Ignore the lane to your left and then fork RIGHT up a short hill to a T-junction where you turn RIGHT. You will head towards Porth Clais, and shortly you go down a hill to the little harbour, where it's well worth stopping to have a look.

7. After looking at the harbour climb on up the hill out of Porth Clais to the cross-roads.

8. At the cross-roads, go STRAIGHT on towards a picturesque farm on your right (only joking) and Clegyr-Boia. Go down the hill passing Pwl Trefeiddan lake on your left, just a reed bed in the Summer, to a T-junction.

9. At the T-junction turn LEFT, and head towards St Justinian's Life Boat station at the bottom of the hill and the wonderful view of Ramsey Island across the Sound.

10. Return the way you came up the hill. Ignore the road to your left signposted "Private Road."

11. (O.R.S) Take the next LEFT turning towards Carn Poeth Farm, sign-posted as a 'No Through road'. At Upper Treleddyn Farm go STRAIGHT through the farm. Ignore the track to your left and go straight on past the buildings. Fork RIGHT onto a bridleway. Half way along this bridleway you will come to a wet section; don't be tempted to try to ride through the large puddle as it is deep in the middle. I found this out to my cost and had wet feet for the rest of the ride. It is only wet after a long spell of rain. Ride on to a metalled road section. Carry on past Whitesands Bay Hotel and a golf course on your left to a cross-roads. You can turn left down the steep hill to Whitesands Bay – about 1 mile – sit on the beach, eat an ice-cream and sun-bathe before carrying on with your journey.

12. (R.S.) At the cross-roads, go STRAIGHT on over (don't forget, if you have been down to Whitesands Bay, to turn left) – this is a slightly left stagger. Continue onwards ignoring the turnings to

Trefelly Farm and the Youth Hostel on your left, and pass a caravan park on your right. Cycle on to a T-junction.

13. At the T-junction turn LEFT and ignore the left fork to Treleddyd-fawr Farm. Keep on this lane disregarding all left turns until you come to a T-junction.

14. At the T-junction turn LEFT. Ignore the first turning right and cycle on for about ½ mile; pass the Hendre Eynon Horse Centre or Caravan Park on your right – grid reference 772 281, to the next road on your right.

15. At this road turn RIGHT. This is an unfenced lane that goes past Treiago Farm, and across Treiago Moor and Wern Moor. These are both protected rare stretches of wet land owned by the National Trust.

16. At the fork, go RIGHT and cross Tretio Common, ignoring the road to your left. Pass an old school or church on your left, which has been converted into a house. Carry on to the main A487 road.

17. At the main road turn LEFT and turn RIGHT at Boncath Cross. This lane is a long descent down into the valley where you cross over the River Solva. Climb up the hill past Caerforiog Farm on your left.

18. After the farm, take the next RIGHT turning and go down the hill to the Woollen Mill on your right.

19. Pass the mill, go over the bridge and turn RIGHT at the T-junction. Take the LEFT turning to Whitchurch up a steep hill (not the road sign posted to Solva).

20. Keep on this road with the old Airfield on your right. Ignore the road to your right and the two roads to your left. When the road bends left fork RIGHT (almost straight on) and follow on alongside the airfield. After you swing right round the last runway you will go down a hill, and as the road starts to climb, fork LEFT.

21. After a longish climb, you will soon reach the main A487 road. Turn RIGHT and within ½ mile you will reach the car park on your left where you started. You may like to carry straight on and enter the city of St David's, have a drink at the local pub or just wander round the Cathedral and the many quaint little shops.

St David's

St David's is a little village which is also the smallest city in Britain. It may seem very strange that such a small place boasts its own cathedral but St David's was an important place of pilgrimage. The original church was founded by St David – the Patron Saint of Wales – in the 6th century but nothing survives of the original structure. The existing structure dates from the 12th to 16th centuries.

The cathedral has undergone much rebuilding and extension since its conception; the work has been funded from the offerings of pilgrims at the shrine of St David. There are several architectural styles. The cathedral was built on marshy ground and so during the 15th century buttresses had to be built to support the leaning nave

St David's Cathedral

walls. At this time a wooden roof was added under the instruction of William Pole.

During the Reformation, pilgrimages were discouraged and the cathedral was left to fall into disrepair. Parts of the cathedral were left to ruin and the adjoining Bishops Palace was abandoned. In 1860 however, Sir George Gilbert Scott set about restoring the cathedral, and restoration work has continued until today. The cathedral is now a resplendent site for visitors to admire.

Clegyr Boia

Clegyr Boia is the site of an Iron Age hill fort and Neolithic settlement. It measures 320ft long by 100ft wide. Most of the facing stones have been removed for building purposes and are an integral part of some local houses.

It was constructed in the 6th century and was occupied by Boia, a chieftain who was a considerable source of annoyance to St David, and was said to have tempted him with nubile women. History maintains that he resisted, and in retribution – so the legend goes – St David destroyed the fortress by causing fire to fall from Heaven. On the site there is reputed to be a small well just big enough to put one's fist in and it was claimed that the water from this well healed sore eyes.

St Nons Chapel and Well

The small ruined cliff-top chapel of St Nons was said to be the birth place of St David. The chapel was dedicated to his mother Non. A short distance up the hill from the ruined chapel is a small vaulted holy well to which pilgrims travelling to St David's stopped in the hope that the holy water would cure their ills. The money that the devout gave at the well was taken to the cathedral and shared out amongst the Canons, who no doubt felt better for it.

St Justinian's and the Chapel

St Justinian's chapel was another chapel belonging to St David's but unlike St Nons there is still a substantial amount surviving. It was built by Bishop Vaughan in the 16th Century and overlooks Ramsey Island, which is where St Justinian is said to have been murdered by his followers who became tired of his sanctimonious ways.

The lifeboat is stationed at St Justinian's and was the location for the television series "The Lifeboat." The seas around here can become very treacherous as you will see if you cycle down on a windy winter day. Throughout time there have been many wrecks off this coast in the notorious Ramsey Sound.

How was it for us?

We have included this ride simply because it would be a crime to come to Pembrokeshire and not visit St David's. This is an area of mystic and magic; of goblins, magicians, myths, legends and, of course, Saints. It is not until you have parked the car and walked or ridden around this beautiful peninsular that you begin to fully appreciate its unique charm.

So on a mild spring day we set off for St David's. Today, there were only four of us; the boys, Ben and Tom, were playing football. We parked in the car park on the outskirts of St David's city and headed out of the back entrance past the toilet block, trying them as we passed; what a relief to find they were open! Soon out of the car park, we headed along the lane to Caerfi bay. We turned right onto a narrow gravelled bridle-path that led us past a new housing estate and on towards the older part of St David's. After a couple of right turns we were in the centre of the city at the Cross Square. From here we turned sharp left down an old narrow cobbled lane, passed under the ancient gateway and there before us in the valley stood St David's Cathedral. I have visited St David's Cathedral on many occasions and I am still struck by its timeless beauty.

We rode down the hill and came to the ford that runs alongside the Bishops Palace. There is a perfectly good foot-bridge across the ford but to use it would be cheating; anyway John and I love a challenge. I plunged into the ford, peddled steadily across and made it to the other side without wet feet. It was John's turn – with great deliberation he set off across the gurgling stream. All was well until he reached the middle, then he lost it. The bike slipped and John had to plunge both of his feet into the water to stop falling off the bike. With Jill and Barbara and most of the visitors to St David's all watching and laughing from the foot-bridge, John waded across the ford.

After our water sports we climbed the steep little hill away from the cathedral and turned left onto the road. Before long, after a left and a couple of rights, we were heading down the hill to Porth Clais. At Porth Clais, a pretty little fishing harbour, we stopped for a few minutes to watch a shipwright making repairs to an old wooden boat. We dragged ourselves away and started the first long climb on the ride out of the valley. At the top of the hill we headed straight on at a cross-roads and before us on a hilly crag stood Clegyr-Boia Settlement, once an important Chieftain's fortress. With a scruffy farm lying in its shelter, it looked more like a scrap merchant's yard than a proud ancient monument.

Soon we were descending again and on our left was Pwl Trefeiddan lake complete with reed beds and wild fowl. Today it did look like a lake but, in the middle of the summer after a dry spell, it completely disappears; except for the reed beds you wouldn't know it was there. At the next road junction we turned left and headed across the flat moor land towards St Justinian's and Ramsey Island. The road climbed and suddenly plunged down towards the sea. Here the view was simply breathtaking and it was hard to keep your eyes on the road as we speeded down the hill.

What a picturesque place St Justinian's is, with the Life Boat Station, the old ruin of the Abbey and the wonderful view out over Ramsey Sound. So we sat on the grassy bank with the warm spring sun on our faces and started to devour our welcome lunch. It was here that Barbara noticed the plastic bag that held John's sandwiches. Printed in big letters on the front were the words 'Poopa Scupa Bag' – what a bag to wrap your sandwiches in, a good job it wasn't a used one.

After we finished lunch, we headed back the way we came, up the hill, until we reached the left turning to Carn Poeth Farm. Soon we passed through the farm buildings and we were on a muddy bridleway. The path was rough and very muddy after all the rain we had in the past week. All went well until I reached a very large puddle, which completely blocked the path. I went for it, straight through the middle, which usually works out fine, but not today. When I reached the middle, the water suddenly changed from being six inches deep to more like three foot deep and I lost it. It was my turn to wade out of the muddy water, my only consolation was that I didn't have such a large audience watching. After this, the going became quite easy and all we could hear was the song of the birds and the squelching of my feet in my boots.

When we reached the road we headed on across the cross-roads and cycled on down narrow winding lanes. The countryside here was flat and easy, and with beautiful views of the sea, Carn Lidi and Carn Perfedd on our left, we cycled along in complete bliss. After a few miles we crossed Tretio Common, an ancient wet land protected by the National trust. As we crossed the common two buzzards circled lazily above us their cries sounding like that of a kitten calling out for its mother. When we reached the main road we headed straight across and soon we were descending towards Solva River. This was the best descent of the ride and we made the most of it, trying to milk every last bit of speed out of our bikes. Down in the valley we crossed over the river and started our climb up the other side. We turned right at the top and after a short stretch we were heading downhill again towards Middle Mill. At the bottom of the hill we passed the Woollen Mill on our right, crossed over the river bridge and turned left up the hill towards Whitchurch and St David's. After all the easy riding so far, this hill is quite a shock: it seemed to go on for ever, and it was with lungs bursting and legs aching that we reached the summit and the flat plain of St David's.

With only a few miles left of our journey we cycled across the old war-time airfield, now just a crumbling criss-cross of old runways. In no time at all we were at the main road. We turned right and soon reached the car park where we had started our journey this morning. It was nice to change my socks back at the car, but it really had been a pleasant ride around St David's peninsula.

Ride 11: Poppit Sands and St Dogmael's

Abbreviations: O.R.S. Off-road Section; R.S. Road Section.

Distance: 10 miles.

Time: 3 hours.

Terrain: Medium. Country lanes and bridleways; one really hard climb.

Map: Ordnance Survey Outdoor Leisure 35 North Pembrokeshire.

Start and finish: At the car park by Poppit Sands. Grid Reference 154 485.

---

1. (R.S) Leave the car park at the same entrance which you entered by and turn RIGHT into the lane (not the coast road). Ride on past the caravan site on your left and start the long ascent of the hill. We hope you have been practising your hill climbs because you will need every breath now. Keep on climbing, ignoring the road to your right and the bridleway to Cippyn church. This is on your right by Esgyr-Fawr. Take a breather here, and carry on climbing to the top of the hill at the left-hand bend just past Esgyr-Draw. At the bend ignore the track to your right and ride on along the lane. Ignore the turnings on your right to Granant Isaf Farm, Granant Uchaf Farm and Penlan Farm. Soon you will be at Pantygroes House on your left, and a road to your right.

2. Turn RIGHT, grid reference 132 462. Follow this lane passing the Cemetery on your right to a sharp right-hand bend and Gilfach Farm on your left.

3. (O.R.S) This is where you turn LEFT and follow the bridleway signs. Ride along this track, ignoring the track to your right to a gate at Pantsaeson Farm. Go through this gate and the track turns LEFT; the farm buildings are on your right. Ahead of you is another gate that enters a very small field which has a gate,

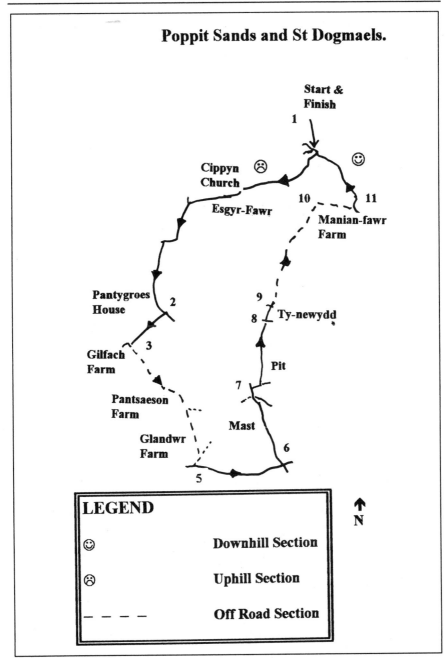

Poppit Sands and St Dogmaels.

Start & Finish

1

Cippyn ☹
Church

10   11

Esgyr-Fawr   Manian-fawr Farm

Pantygroes House   2   9

Gilfach   3   8   Ty-newydd
Farm

Pit

Pantsaeson   7
Farm

Mast
Glandwr   6
Farm

5

LEGEND

☺   Downhill Section

☹   Uphill Section

— — — —   Off Road Section

↑
N

in front and to your right, across the field. Go through both of these gates and you will find yourself in a narrow muddy lane. Ride along this muddy lane to yet another gate and a fork in the tracks, fork RIGHT here.

4. Still on the bridleway, proceed straight on ignoring tracks to your right and your left, to a road to your right to Glandwr Farm, marked with a footpath sign. Go STRAIGHT on through a gate and cross two fields by an old green lane to another gate. Go through the gate and turn RIGHT following the edge of the field to a gate by the road.

5. (R.S) At the road turn LEFT and climb the hill. Soon the hill levels out and you reach a cross-roads.

6. When you reach the cross-roads turn LEFT and cycle on passing a radio mast on your left. Go down a hill and go STRAIGHT on at the cross-roads until you soon reach the first road on your right.

7. Turn RIGHT and then turn LEFT by a disused pit on your right. Climb up the narrow lane then go down the hill to the cross-roads.

8. At the cross-roads go STRAIGHT on, pass Ty-newydd on your right and you come to a T-junction.

9. (O.R.S) Here you go STRAIGHT on down a narrow track. This track marked as a 'Road used as a Public Footpath' on the map is very overgrown in places with high hedges on either side, but just head on, you can get through. The track descends to a battered old gate. Go through the gate into a large field. Go STRAIGHT on across the field to a gate you can see in the distance. Go through the gate onto a metalled track and go down to another gate by Manian Fawr Farm.

10. Go through the gate, and turn RIGHT down the lane and cycle on to a T-junction.

11. (R.S.) When you reach the T-junction turn LEFT onto the B4546, go down the hill and soon you will see the River Teifi estuary on your right. Cycle on to the road and the car park on your LEFT where you started your journey.

How was it for us?

The St Dogmael's peninsular is extremely beautiful and quite rugged, where everything is shaped by the constantly blowing westerly wind. Yet there are secluded wooded valleys and lush pastures that nestle to the lee of the wind. The coast line has wonderful craggy cliffs, where seals breed and choughs fly. In the winter this can be a hard place to live. From November to March the westerly gales roar in from the Atlantic bending any trees left standing to its will. This can be very useful if you get lost because all the trees lean in an easterly direction. If you can put up with the gales and the rain that lashes at you like pellets from a shotgun, you will love this place. In the summer months this place is heaven, washed by the gulf stream and warmed by the long sunny days.

Preparing for the ride, Poppit Sands

Though this ride is only about ten miles long, don't be fooled into thinking that it is going to be easy. The first hill alone will test your strength and endurance; after that you will have to cope with an off-road downhill section that will certainly test your riding skills.

Barbara and I set off on a warm Saturday in June to complete this ride. We parked in the car park by Poppit Sands and turned right onto the narrow lane that headed away from the sea. At first, the lane started to climb gradually, but then it started to head straight up the side of the mountain. It's not so bad when you have been cycling for a while and your muscles are warm, but this can be quite a slog. We persevered up the hill until we reached the little Chapel of Cippyn by Esgyr-Fawr. Already we had climbed 125m from sea level and our legs and chest felt ready for a rest. Staggering into the little lay-by by the Chapel we turned to look at the scenery from where we had ridden. Down below us the River Teifi glittered in the estuary, and the sands of Poppit were a rich golden colour against the blue of the sea flooding in on the tide. Away in the distance we could make out the mountains of Mid Wales shimmering in the summer heat.

After this excuse to look at the scenery we set off again up the hill. This last section of road seemed even steeper than the previous stretch if that was possible, and it took every ounce of strength to haul ourselves to the top. At last, the road levelled out and we had reached the summit by the turning to Grant-uchaf Farm. We had climbed 195m from sea level and covered 3 mile straight up, and our legs knew it. We stopped to take some photographs with a back drop of the sea and the vibrant yellow of the flowering gorse. The lane meandered along through a flat landscape criss-crossed with high hedges that were a blaze of colour from the early summer flowers.

At Pantygroes House we turned right and cycled on passing a small cemetery to our right. This spot, on both sides of the road, has been used as a burial ground since the Iron Age so even today the locals are still keeping with an ancient tradition. When we reached a right-hand bend in the road by Gilfach Farm, we turned left onto a metalled bridleway. Within a short distance the track became rough and bumpy so we rode on until we reached a gate at Pantsaeson Farm. We passed through the gate and took a left through another gate which took us across a small field that skirted around the old farm buildings. One more gate lay in our path, which we passed though into a narrow muddy lane, hemmed in by two large hedges. Here the mud was deep, thick and smelly from the cattle that had used it earlier, so it was important not to lose your balance and have to wade through the smelly mire. At the end of the lane we passed through two gates and forked right down a wider bridleway. This flat track headed straight on between the hedgerows until we reached an iron field gate. The bridleway crossed into an old green roadway that crossed the open fields, so we rode along accompanied by the playful sheep until we reached the road.

Turning left on to the road we cycled up a short hill until we came to a cross-roads. Bordered on both sides by open fields we turned left into a lane and started a slight descent. At a grassy clearing by a cross-roads we decided to sit in the sun and have our lunch. This was a peaceful spot, the silence disturbed only by the bleating of the sheep and the occasional squawk of the large crows in the trees. Time drifted slowly past in this idyllic place, but we had to move on.

Going straight on at the cross-roads, we took a right turn and then a left into a narrow grassy lane. To our right was the site of a disused colliery, overgrown and long forgotten, and unrecognisable except for a small tree-clad mound. The lane slowly climbed upwards and as we went over the brow of the hill, so the panorama of the Teifi estuary opened out before us. A gentleman panting and sweating came pushing his bike up the hill towards us. "Bit warm today" he exclaimed, we agreed and stood for a good half hour discussing the weather, the beer at the local inn and, of course, rugby. To live in Wales and not to talk about rugby is a crime. It is almost a religion, with Cardiff Arms Park as the cathedral in which to sing songs of praise to the men in red.

Waving farewell, we parted and sped off in different directions, like ships that pass in the night. We went straight over a cross-roads and reached an overgrown track that is actually listed as a road on the map. Luckily the track descends so all you have to do is hang on tight, dodge the overhanging branches, miss the tentacle tree roots and hope you don't get stung on the stinging nettles. Lose concentration for one second and you will be plunged headlong into the stingers and the thorn bushes, but who cares; this is what real mountain biking is all about. Eventually we reached an old rusty over-grown field gate at the end of the track, which we managed to open and close without it falling off its hinges. According to the map the road is supposed to head straight across the open fields to Manian Fawr Farm at the bottom of the valley, not that you can see any sign of the road on the ground. We headed down into the valley, passed through two gates and emerged on a lane by the farm buildings.

Turning right onto the lane we cycled on until we reached a T-junction at the B4546. We turned left and slowly ambled along the last leg of our journey. The road was flat as it ran alongside the River Teifi Estuary, and so we slowly cycled onwards in the late evening sun, until we reached the car park on our left where we started our journey. A fine way to finish a wonderful afternoon in the sun.

Mynydd Preseli: the Region

A Brief History

Mynydd Preseli, or the Preseli Hills as they are called in English, are in northern Pembrokeshire to the South east of Newport and south-west of Cardigan. These hills can be quite menacing in the middle of winter if the mist comes down and it would be a foolish person who ventured onto them without spare clothing, a map and a compass. They are not very high in terms of mountains, but still need to be treated with respect as it is very easy to get lost on them, and you can soon get very cold!

Four hundred million years ago, during the Silurian Period, a great mountain range was thrown up. These hills are all that remain from the combined effects of erosion and the retreat of the last glaciers some 8000 years ago. Many of the rocks are magnetic and can have strange effects on your compass, so be warned!

The highest point of the Preseli hills is Foel Cwm Cerwyn which rises to 537m (grid reference 094 312) and is otherwise known as Preseli Top. The ridge of the Preseli hills runs from Foel Eryr in the west to Crymych in the east and all along this ridge on either side many cairns are to be found. These are constructed of heaps of dark grey Bluestone rock of the type used to build the Bluestone circle and the Bluestone horseshoe of Stonehenge. It is believed that stones from here, 82 in total and weighing an average of 4 tons each, were transported by land and sea to Stonehenge – a distance of about 180 miles. During the 1970s, Professor Atkinson of the University of Wales conducted an experiment to find out whether it would have been possible for Bronze Age man to have accomplished this task. Setting up a system of wooden rollers and with the help of 14 schoolchildren he was able to move a 4 ton slab.

The many cairns dotted across the Preseli hills were the burial places of important Bronze Age people. These burial places tended to be in conspicuous places such as hilltops or ridges where they stood out against the skyline, giving a strange and eerie look to the landscape. Seeing them protruding from the mist today, we can understand how powerful and magical they must have appeared to Bronze Age people.

Dotted over the Preseli hills are many examples of standing stones, some of which are set in circles as in the case of Gors Fawr which stands on moorland approximately 1000m west of Mynachlog-ddu (grid reference 133 292). There are at least seventy standing stones in Pembrokeshire with most of them in the north and of Bronze Age origin. It is believed that some stones may have served as waymarkers on ancient tracks while others may have marked burial places. Along the wayside you will see small stones, of much later origin, with initials carved on them. These are said to be the gravestones of drovers who died along the way while transporting their cattle.

During the Iron Age, around 1,000 BC many hill forts and defended settlements were constructed. Excellent examples of these are Foel Drygarn (grid reference 157 336) on the eastern tip of the Preseli Ridge and Carn Ingli on the summit of a rocky outcrop 337m above sea level, and about 2 miles south of Newport. Foeldrygarn which means "the bare hill of the three cairns" is very appropriately named because within its perimeter are three cairns of the earlier Bronze Age period.

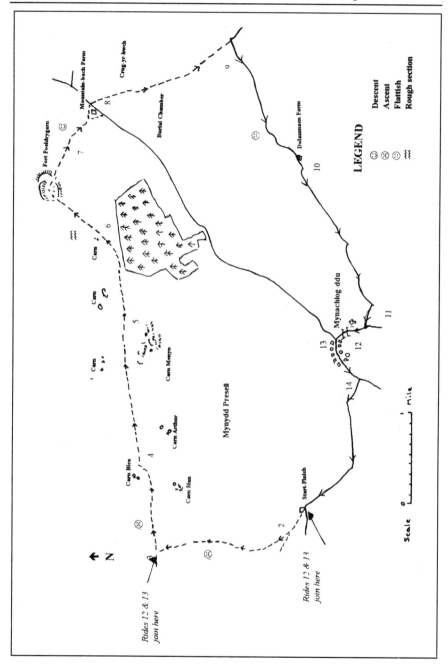

Ride 12: Mynydd Preseli, among the Carns

Abbreviations: O.R.S. Off-road Section; R.S. Road Section.

Distance: 11 Miles.

Time: 2 – 3 hours.

Terrain: Some steep climbs, fairly difficult.

Map: Ordnance Survey Outdoor Leisure 35.

Start: At car park 1½ mile west of Mynachlogddu, Grid Reference 127 306. The car park is on a bend in the road, with Dan-y-garn farm to the east and Pantithel farm to the south-west.

This ride takes in some of the highest points in the Preseli hills, visiting the magic carns of Menym and Drygarn from where the Blue Stones of Stonehenge originated.

The Ride

1. Leave the car park by bridle path heading NORTH-WEST, round the west side of Graig Tailfyndd mountain. Ignore the track forking off to the left. The bridlepath gets boggy in places but keep heading north.

2. At about a mile into the ride you will cross an old drovers' trail heading west to east. Turn RIGHT on to the trail, heading due EAST, and start to climb up a steep hill towards Carn Sian which you can't see until you reach the top.

3. From Carn Sian, grid reference 128 321, follow the path NORTH-EAST towards Carn Menyn passing Carn Bica on your left and Carn Arthur on your right.

4. At Carn Menyn, grid reference 144 325, climb to the top and look out towards the rolling hills and valleys of South Pembrokeshire.

This is where the Blue stones of Stonehenge were cut and transported across Wales and England to their resting place. A good time to sit, have a break and contemplate on how the Druids accomplished this feat

5. Strike off on the path heading NORTH-EAST towards Carn Foel Drygarn Iron Age fort and settlement; grid reference 158 337. The path disappears in places, so just head across the heather in a straight line towards Foel Drygarn.

6. From Carn Foel Drygarn head SOUTH-EAST on a path that goes downhill towards a gate at Mountain-bach farm at the corner of the field fence, just before the burial chamber at Crug-yr-hwch.

7. Go through the gate and take the lane to the LEFT

8. At the road, go STRAIGHT across through the gate and follow the old road which is a bridle path. Ignore the track on the right. After about a mile on the old road, you come to a gate at a road. Turn RIGHT onto the road and head towards Dolaumaen Farm.

9. Keep on the road passing Llwyn-drain Farm, Dolaumaen Farm, Dolau-newydd and on towards Mynachlog-ddu.

10. At a T-junction by Maes-yr wyn house, turn RIGHT. The day we passed eight red setter dogs tried to scale the fence to bark at us, luckily it was a high fence.

11. Enter Mynachlog-ddu; pass the church and cemetery on the right. Go over river bridge.

12. At T-junction turn LEFT, ride on past the Post Office.

13. At the next road, about 200m past the post office, take a RIGHT fork and head due east to the car park where you started.

Fort Foeldrygarn

This was originally the site of 3 large Bronze Age burial mounts but later a hill fort was established here. It is still possible to trace the foundations of the old dwellings on the hilltop.

Carn Menyn

The great slabs of "bluestone", which are actually spotted dolomite, are reputed to have been hauled from here to build Stonehenge.

How was it for us?

Pembrokeshire is a strange county. In the south it bustles with holiday makers for most of the summer season, but for some reason the wilder north is almost forgotten. Straddled across the north lie the Preseli Mountains, Mynydd Preseli in Welsh. These aren't high mountains, the highest being only 536m but they have a haunting magical charm about them. They are Merlin's mountains, with names like Carn Arthur, Carn Bica and Carn Menyn. Dotted with standing stones, druids' circles and Iron Age forts, it's a wonderful place to spend a day.

So one hot day in August we headed from the busy south, where we live, to Mynydd Preseli in North Pembrokeshire, bikes loaded and water bottles filled. A high pressure zone had stationed itself over Wales and now was the time to cross the mountains in perfect weather.

The six of us left the car park at the foot of Craig Tailfyndd mountain and rode north-west on the old bridlepath. Today, the path was rutted and sun-baked, but easier going than in the winter.

We turned right on to the ancient drovers' trail that runs from St David's across the Welsh mountains to England. The hard part began. Under a relentless blue sky, we toiled up the hill, until at last we came to Carn Sian, standing like a proud statue to the gods. With lungs bursting, we all seemed to have things wrong with our bikes. Straps needed tightening, rucksacks needed adjusting, anything to stop and get our breath, but we didn't catch our breath for long: the view soon took it away again. To the north in a blue haze we could make out the mountains of Mid Wales and to the west the white flecked blue of the Irish sea, beckoning us to cool our feet in its waters.

With mind and body suitably rested we set off towards Carn Arthur and Carn Menyn. Here at last on the mountain ridge the going was easier. At Carn Menyn we stopped and decided that this was the ideal place for our picnic. We parked at the foot of the Carn, no need to lock the bikes here today as we had only seen two lonely walkers and there was no chance of someone sneaking up and stealing our cherished chariots. Off we all scrambled to the top of Carn Menyn and selected suitable stones for our picnic tables. Over lunch we discussed, with some incredible suggestions, how the Druids had moved the huge stones from here to Stonehenge.

Coming down was just that bit harder. Why is it that sheep have this nasty habit of depositing packages in all the places that you need to place either your hands or your feet, and how did the sheep manage to get up here in the first place? Definitely no pooper scoopers here!

From Carn Menyn we headed in a North easterly direction towards Carn

Among the Carns

Foel Drygarn, an Iron Age fort and settlement. The path that we took was narrow and in places it totally disappeared making control through the heather quite difficult but fun. We just pointed our bikes at Foel Drygarn in the distance and went for it.

Before long Drygarn loomed up in front of us, much larger close up than we thought it would be. With much effort we climbed as high as we could into the fort before riding our bikes became impossible. From the top the Preseli Mountains cascaded down towards the sleepy Welsh town of Crymych, way down in the valley. This was a town untouched for years except by a '60s comprehensive school that stood out like a sore thumb; the sun reflecting from its walls of windows.

We headed south-east on a path downhill towards a gate at Mountain-bach Farm and the road below. Hang on tight and enjoy the ride. This is what mountain biking is all about!

We passed through the gate and took the lane to our left, skirting around the farm buildings. In a few minutes we were at the road, were we met a farmer who looked as surprised to see us as we were to see him. "Nice day for a bike ride," he remarked, "We don't see many people up here on bikes." Most Welsh people love to pass the time of day and are really hurt if you hurry past them without even a nod. It doesn't cost anything to have a chat, and it will make your life that much richer.

After a few minutes of exchanging pleasantries we crossed over the road through the iron gate and continued along an old bridle path with the TV mast on the mountain almost straight ahead. The going was easy, almost a flat surface, with no problems except for the sheep who seemed to want to play kamikaze pilots every few hundred metres.

Soon we were at our next turning; passing through yet another gate we turned right down a narrow leafy lane towards Dolaumaen Farm. At the T-junction by Maes-yr-wyn house we turned right. The day we passed eight red setter dogs tried to scale a thankfully high fence to bark at us. Here, we seemed to find the energy to race on up the road.

Within minutes we were entering the little village of Mynachlog-ddu, passing the church and crossing over the river bridge. Turning left towards the post office, we rode through the village; not that we found the post office, but it must be there because it says so on the map. No sweets or ice cream here today.

Just outside the village we took the first right fork and headed east back on the road to the car park where we started our journey. We were hot, dusty and tired but we had really enjoyed our ride among the Carns of Mynydd Preseli.

Ride 13: Preseli Mountains from Rosebush

Abbreviations: O.R.S. Off-road Section; R.S. Road Section.

Distance: 11 miles.

Time: 2 – 3 hours.

Terrain: Bridleways and country lanes.

Map: Outdoor Leisure Map 36 North Pembrokeshire.

Start and finish: At the car park at the rear of the Old Post office in Rosebush. Grid Reference 075 295.

1. Leave the car park and turn LEFT onto the lane that heads towards the mountains with the cottages on your left. Ride on down the lane past the cottages, and then the road quickly becomes an unsurfaced track. Pass by the old Rosebush Quarry workings on your right and soon you will come to a metal field gate. Pass through the gate and ignore the track to your left and carry STRAIGHT on with the trees to your left. Soon you will enter the woods with trees on both sides of the track and you start to climb upwards. When the track starts to go round a long right-hand bend, you pass two electric poles on your left. The road bears left: look out for a narrow path forking off to your left across a stream – take care here or you can miss this turning.

2. Fork LEFT onto the narrow path and cross over the stream. Soon you exit the wood and the path follows a fence on your left. There is open moorland to your left, with trees on your right, and beyond the trees, felled woodland. The track starts to get steeper with every turn of the pedals. Just after you pass a permissive footpath going off to your left, the path climbs sharply and meets another wider track coming from the right.

3. Turn LEFT and follow the track ever upwards. Ignore lesser tracks to your left and your right and carry on to a fork in the tracks.

4. Fork LEFT and climb an even steeper track until you again reach another fork in the tracks (look out for an old wooden footpath sign up on a bank to the right of the track, which you must take).

5. Fork LEFT again, and ride on a narrower track that climbs through the trees to a field gate (stile) that passes onto the open mountain side at Bwich Pennant.

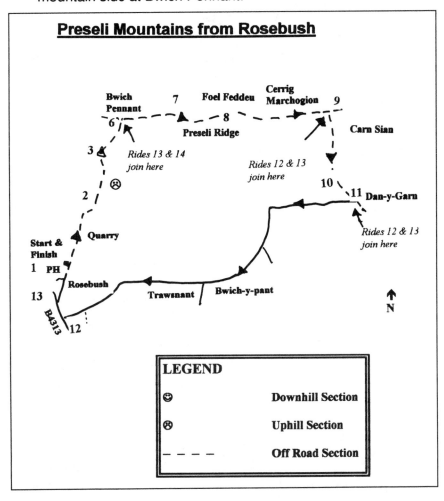

Preseli Mountains from Rosebush

LEGEND

☺   **Downhill Section**

⊗   **Uphill Section**

– – – –   **Off Road Section**

6. After you have got your breath back, pass through the gate and turn RIGHT in an easterly direction onto a track that runs parallel to the forest on your right. You are on the Preseli Ridge on the Pilgrims Way (or Robbers' Road). This is the ancient track that has been used for thousands of years.

7. Soon you leave the forest on your left and start to cross the open mountain side. Keep on the track heading east as the track starts to descend. You will see in the distance the carns of Foel Feddeu. The track soon starts to climb up to this point and at the top (467m) you have a wonderful view across the surrounding mountains.

8. Leave Foel Feddeu and descend in an easterly direction, keeping to the narrow rough track. Ahead of you to your right are the standing stones of Cerrig Marchogion. Cycle on past these ancient stones and go down into a valley to a track coming from your right.

9. Turn RIGHT onto this track and ride south with the mountain of Carn Sian on your left. The track skirts around the side of the mountain and carries on to a track to your right.

10. Ignore this track and keep riding in a south-easterly direction to the road and car park at Dan-y-garn.

11. At the road turn RIGHT and follow this quiet lane ignoring all roads to your left and right. Pass by Glynaerton, a small farm on your left. Continue, passing the farms of Bwlch-y-pant, Trawsnant, Mae-llwyd and Mount Pleasant to the B4313.

12. Turn RIGHT at the B4313 and cycle down the hill to the second road on your right sign-posted to Rosebush.

13. Here you turn RIGHT and cycle along the lane to the turning on your left that takes you to the car-park where you started your journey.

Rosebush

The railway, built during 1872 to 1876, led to a new slate quarry complex being established at Rosebush. There was an abundance of high quality dark blue slate which had been created by the intrusion of igneous rocks into the local shales.

The slate quarry was owned by Sir Huw Owen, an eccentric gentleman who convinced himself that Rosebush would become a holiday resort. He set about creating artificial lakes and stocking them with fish and lily plants. He built the Precelly Hotel to house all the visitors, but he waited in vain, for none came.

Today Rosebush is a quaint little village, though not exactly pretty it exudes a charm all of its own. An unsurfaced road leads to the derelict quarries. The old Post Office is now a Bistro and Visitor Centre. If you go down the lane and round to the back of the Public House you will find the old railway station, much tarted up for the benefit of the visitors. It is now the Beer Garden of the green corrugated building which was the Preseli Hotel and has later been named the Tafarn Sinc.

Although Rosebush is not busy even at the height of the season, people are beginning to discover this charming little place and the mystical hills of Preseli that watch over it.

How was it for us?

The weather forecast was excellent for the weekend so Barbara and I decided to head for the hills and complete another ride over the Preseli Mountains. We awoke early on Saturday and looked out of the window. The sky was a clear cloudless blue and out over the sea only small flecks of white could be seen which meant that there was not too much wind – the perfect day. For early September the weather was still warm, but because we know how changeable it can be in the Preselis, we packed our fleeces and Pertex waterproofs, just in case.

Rosebush is a strange little place set at the bottom of the mountain, a place where time has stood still since the quarries closed; with its disused station, the Post Office, the Inn and the one row of workers' cottages painted in pastel colours that Dulux would be proud of. We parked in the car-park at the rear of the old Post Office and set off in a good mood. Immediately we turned left onto the narrow flat lane and headed for the mountain in front of us. We cycled along passing the workers cottages on our left and very soon we came to the disused slate quarry on our right. Huge piles of stones towered above us with the broken pieces of slate keyed together like the pyramids of ancient Egypt. Nature was taking back this effigy of man's destruction; small trees were clinging to the steep walls and grass was starting to grow in the sheltered

Sometimes, you just have to get off and push!

hollows. Fleet footed sheep scampered up and down bleating to each other, as we had the cheek to ride past and disturb their breakfast feed. You could believe that you were on the rim of some long ago extinct volcano with a strange tormented beauty. High above on the mountain white cloud seemed to appear like magic out of a blue sky and roll across the summit.

After leaving the quarry we came to an iron field gate across the track, which had a convenient opening on its left side to walk or ride through. Ignoring the track on our left, we set off along a track that wound its way through a pine forest. The track began to climb, gradually at first and then a little steeper. Slowly we rode around a long right-hand bend and passed on our left two wooden poles carrying high voltage electricity. Just after passing the poles the track veered left and it was here we noticed the narrow path off to the left. If we hadn't been awake we could have easily missed this turning and headed on into the forest.

Splashing across the small stream we started to ride along a narrow path that followed a fence to our left. The path started to ascend at a steady rate and we climbed up a steep bank to meet a track coming from our right. To the right the forest had been felled in a recent logging operation and neatly cut trees lay in tidy piles exhaling a smell of sweet pine. The track became a steady slog as we climbed through the forest with lungs bursting and legs aching. It was much colder and a sharp west wind was blowing through the trees and the occasional grey cloud was lumbering across the mountain top. We forked left twice and then we rode along a narrow track, that at last started to level out. Soon we reached a fence and a gate, passed through it and cycled onto the open mountainside. A track went to our left and right; this was the ancient Pilgrims or Robbers Road that crosses over the Preseli Mountains from St David's to Crymych.

This old roadway has many names including Flemings Way, Pilgrims Way and the lurid Robbers Road. It has been in use since the Iron Age, linking the many barrows, burial sites and hillside forts that straddle the Preselis. In later times it was used as a trail by Drovers who took their large herds of cattle to the markets in the cities of England. You can still see today the initialled small grave stones that stand beside the road in memory of these hardy men who lost their lives when they crossed these lonely and dangerous mountains.

We turned right onto the old road in blazing sunshine and the view was tremendous across to Carn Ingli and the sea at Newport. As we rode on suddenly the wind increased and the sun disappeared as a wall of mist swirled across the mountain top. No wonderful view now! It was only possible to see about thirty metres in any direction. It really was cold, so we put on our extra fleeces and Pertex wind tops to keep out the damp and the chill. In the mist the mountain seemed strange, featureless and unreal. We knew that on our right only metres away lay the forest, but it had vanished into the increasing gloom. Slowing to walking pace we kept to the track which followed the fence bordering the forest. All too soon we came to a fork in the track and we knew that we had to leave the fence behind and follow the track across the open mountain. Like a drowning man leaving his sinking boat we left the fence, took a compass bearing and plunged into the mist.

The track narrowed and started to climb, small boulders loomed out of the mist to make our riding even more difficult as we tried to weave our way along the path. Breathlessly we climbed ever onwards through this surreal landscape. Suddenly on our right a Carn appeared like magic out of the swirling mist, we had reached the summit of Foel Feddau. Pausing to get our breath we sat among a pile of dolomite stones, ate some lunch and peered out into the grey mist. It was their voices we heard first slowly coming towards us from below and two ghostly shapes emerged from the fog. They were as startled to see us as we were to see them. "Do you know where we are? Which way is the car park at the main road?" was all the young couple could say. After we showed them the direction and the track to take, they thanked us and disappeared again into the mist. I hope the directions were correct or they may still be wandering around the mountainside today.

Leaving Foel Feddau we followed an even narrower path that descended the mountain. Just as quickly as it had arrived so the mist departed, and we were riding again in bright sunlight. Luckily we had been on the correct path but we were at least 200m from where we thought we should have been. It just shows that you can never take the mountains for granted.

As we dropped down into the valley the wind decreased and it was just like the summer's day we had left behind in Saundersfoot three hours ago. Off came the fleeces and windproofs and the only problem was the sun burning our faces, but you can't have it all ways, can you? At the cross-roads of tracks we turned right and headed over a marshy stretch. Occasionally making detours around deep wet patches we rode on with the summit of Carn Sian on our left. Down further to our right in the valley, we could see the isolated farm of Cwn garw. Field boundaries began to appear,then the track to Cwn garw farm, and suddenly we had reached the road at Dan-y-garn.

Turning right onto the road, we cycled along, looking up towards the mountain we had just crossed. Cloud again had spread across its summit shrouding it from view but down here in the valley it was tranquil and serene as we rode on towards Rosebush and the end of our journey. The narrow lane meandered along passing isolated farms. Very occasionally a car slowly passed us, the occupant waving as if to some long lost friend. You still don't come across that many people in this part of the world that you can pass without a word or a wave.

When we reached the B4313 road we turned right down the hill, then right again and headed up the lane to Rosebush. Soon we were at the Post Office, we turned left and cycled into the car park where we had started our journey. The bikes were loaded on the car and then we walked back to the Post Office and staggered into the welcome tea room. Scones, with fresh cream and jam washed down with a large cup of tea, what a wonderful way to end the day!

Ride 14: Foel Eryr and the Gwaun Valley

Abbreviations: O.R.S. Off-road Section; R.S. Road Section.

Distance: 14 miles.

Time: 4 hours.

Terrain: Bridleways and country lanes. Hard.

Map: Outdoor Leisure Map 35 North Pembrokeshire.

Start and finish: At Sychbant picnic site in the Gwaun Valley. Grid Reference 045 350. South of Newport, Pembrokeshire, which is the nearest town.

1. (R.S.) Turn LEFT out of the picnic site. Follow this road that winds through the valley, go around the sharp right-hand bend. Bear left and start to climb the hill; in about 100m you will see a gate and a bridleway sign on your right.

2. (O.R.S.) Go through the iron field gate and start to climb a steep sunken track that winds its way through the trees to the top of the hill. At the top of the hill you will come to another field gate. Go through the gate and continue across an open field keeping to the hedge on your right to another field gate. Pass through this gate and cross over another field to a gate by a road.

3. (R.S.) Pass through the gate and turn RIGHT onto the road. Ride down the hill and pass the large house of Gelifawr on your left. Continue down the hill to a right-hand bend in the road at Pont Gelli Fawr. On your left you will see an iron field gate and a track by a stream.

4. (O.R.S) Go through the gate on to a rough track and cross a stream by either the ford or the narrow footbridge. Follow the track with field boundaries made of large boulders on your right to Gernos-fawr Farm. Bear left past the farm; pass through another gate and enter a narrow, sunken track that climbs up to another iron field gate which you pass through.

5. Enter the field and turn RIGHT and follow a track across 4 fields keeping to the hedge on your right, to Gerrios-fach Farm. Go through a gate, pass between the farm buildings, go through another gate to reach a rough metalled track.

6. Turn RIGHT onto this track and ride across the open moor to a gate at the road by Tafarn-y-bwich.

7. Go through the gate and turn RIGHT on to the B4329 road by the old red Telephone box. Cross over the cattle grid.

There are two ways to continue the ride:

¤ By the road to the top of the hill: (R.S.) Follow the B4329 up the hill to the parking spot at the top of the hill at grid reference 075 321, go past the parking spot for about 50m to a lay-by on your left.

or

¤ (O.R.S.) This is the more difficult way – up the bridleway and across the mountain: climb the hill on the road for about 100m and you will see a rough track going south-south-east up the open mountainside. Follow this track to the top of the mountain at grid reference 085 321, (this track is difficult to follow in places so just head south-south-east to the top). At the top of the mountain you will reach a T-junction of tracks at a fence near to the forest. Turn RIGHT here and cycle on to the road at grid reference 075 321, now turn LEFT and ride down the hill for about 50m to a lay-by on your left.

8. (O.R.S.) Cross over the road and pass onto the open mountainside. Climb up a grassy bank and head 240 degrees (south-south-west) at first along a very narrow path that goes around the mountain. With the summit of Foel Eryr on your right and a small plantation of trees on your left, follow the narrow path and circle around the mountain. Keep to a reasonable height so that you miss Waun-trallwn bog on your left. After a while the path disappears in places, but make your way across the mountainside until you see a fence to your left about 200m below you. Follow the fence descending down the mountain. Just before Pen-lan-wynt Farm the path gets clearer to see, and after the farm it widens into a track. Pass by a disused pit and head down to a gate by the road between Berth Gwynne and Ffynnondici Farms.

9. Pass through the gate and turn RIGHT onto the road. Within 30m you will come to a lane on your left sign posted to Ty-gwyn Farm.

10. (O.R.S) Turn LEFT and ride down the lane to an iron field gate at Penrallt-ddu Farm. Pass through the gate and go past the farm

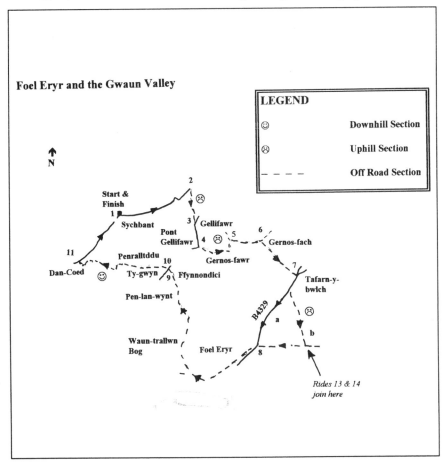

Foel Eryr and the Gwaun Valley

LEGEND

☺   Downhill Section

☹   Uphill Section

— — —   Off Road Section

N

Start & Finish

Sychbant

Pont Gellifawr

Gellifawr

Gernos-fach

Gernos-fawr

Penralltddu

Dan-Coed

Ty-gwyn

Ffynnondici

Tafarn-y-bwlch

Pen-lan-wynt

B4329

Waun-trallwn Bog

Foel Eryr

Rides 13 & 14 join here

buildings, then turn LEFT through another gate and ride down a muddy track. After about 100m turn RIGHT into a narrow overgrown bridleway that runs along the top of a steep valley to your left. Soon you come to a path on your left which you ignore, then the bridleway descends a steep hill on a very rough track. At the bottom of the hill turn LEFT and cross over a footbridge by Dan Coed House; go through a gate and bear right. Pass over another bridge that crosses the Gwaun river and you will quickly reach a T-junction.

11. (R.S.) At the road turn RIGHT and ride on the road through the Gwaun Valley to the picnic site on your left where you started your journey.

Sychbant

This is where you start and finish the ride. There is a very good picnic site here with plenty of space to park your car. Tables to eat your lunch are set in a quiet secluded wooded area alongside a stream. There are also public conveniences. We were very impressed that whatever time of year we go there, they are always open and immaculately clean.

Gwaun Valley

The river Gwaun runs from the Presel hills to Lower Town Fishguard. The valley through which it runs is extremely beautiful having agricultural land along its valley and dense woodland along its steep sides. The woodland is managed for landscape and nature conservation and provides a very pleasant sheltered place to cycle and walk when the winds are howling in along the seashore.

Foel Eryr

Foel Eryr is 468m above sea level, capped with a Bronze Age cairn looking out over Rosebush and Llys-y-fran reservoirs. This is an excellent point to walk up to and enjoy a panoramic view of the area. Don't forget your camera!

How was it for us?

Foel Eryr stood dark and brooding, its peak shrouded in the January mist: not very high at 468m but steep enough when trying to ride our bikes around its boggy side. When we had left home at about 10am the weather was fine but at the Gwaun Valley picnic site, the weather on the mountain didn't look very promising. Today we had some new companions, John and Marie who had decided that they would like to come along for a ride in the Preseli Mountains. For months we had planned to complete this ride, so mist or not, we were going to circle the mountain.

We turned left out of the picnic site and rode along the almost flat lane that meandered beside the River Gwaun. The Gwaun Valley is a beautiful place set between Carn Ingli to the north and Foel Eryr to the south. Sheltered and hidden between the mountains it is a place of perpetual spring, and today it was no different as we cycled along in warm sunshine. After going around a right-hand bend, the road started to climb gently upwards until we reached a field gate that led into a narrow bridleway. The gate was old and rusty; as we opened it, it nearly crashed from its hinges and closing it was a tour de force. Ahead of us the bridleway veered steeply up the valley side between the trees. It was strewn with rocks and boulders and the floor of the bridleway became even more difficult to see because of the deep carpet of fallen leaves. Riding our bikes up this narrow bumpy track was impossible so we pushed and heaved them to the top of the valley. Relieved to be at the top we took a deep breath and rode over three flat open fields until we reached the road.

John and Marie had that look on their faces that said "What have we done, shall we go home now?" I tried to reassure them, because if they could get their bikes up that last hill they could get them anywhere. Somehow I don't think they believed me!

Turning left onto the road we descended to a gate by Pont Gelli Fawr. On the way down the hill, we passed to our left, the beautiful old stone house of Gelifawr, which had been renovated and was up for sale. At the gate we turned left and entered onto a track that crossed a narrow field. We had to cross a small stream, but the water was not very deep so we forded with ease. If the water is deep you can always cross by the rickety old wooden footbridge, if you can get under the trees that have lodged between the wooden rails. The track climbed gently through this old field system, the walls of which were made of huge boulders stacked in a haphazard way. To move some of these stones the builders of the wall must have been incredibly strong – breakfast must have been at least six Weetabix each!

At Gernos-fach Farm we turned left, crossed over a stream and passed through an iron field gate into an old sunken lane. This lane had a stone floor which was rutted with cart tracks and the stones were coated with wet, slippery moss. Climbing at an alarming rate, the lane was impossible to cycle along; each time we tried our wheels just skidded and slipped on the green slime. Even walking was difficult on this section and we slid and slithered to the top of the slope. At the top of the hill we passed through an old iron field gate and turned right into an open grassy field. Gasping for breath we paused and looked back to the fields and the woodland of the Gwaun Valley, lit up by the winter sunshine bursting through the clouds. Then we turned and looked up at the mountain above us, that we still had to climb.

Grateful to be on open countryside we cycled across the fields towards Gernos-fach Farm. When we reached the farm two old Welsh sheep dogs came out barking and snarling at us like the hounds of hell. Fortunately I have never been afraid of dogs – only once have I been bitten by my canine friends, and that was by a Pekinese so old that it had lost all its teeth. After a few words of endearment, the two dogs were wagging their tails and let us pass through their territory without any problem. After the farm we turned right and rode on a metalled track that crossed over the open moorland of Warn Mawn, until we reached the B4329 road and the telephone box at Tafarn-y-bwich.

The old red GPO telephone box stood out like a beacon to sanity by the side of the road; a solid cast-iron box, not one of your modern all glass affairs without a door. In modern telephone boxes you fry in the Summer or freeze to death in the Winter, and to try and hear what somebody is saying to you when a large lorry is passing is simply impossible. Let's hope that this wonderful monument to man's ingenuity is not removed and sold off to be used as a shower cubicle or an object of curiosity. We turned right onto the road, passed by the telephone box and crossed over the cattle grid. We debated which way to continue with our journey. It was a toss up whether to go by road to the top of the hill or to take the hard route across the side of the mountain on the old bridleway. The girls wanted to go by road and Johnny and I wanted to use the bridleway. After a while we chose a compromise: the girls would meet Johnny and I at the top.

Johnny and I set off along the road for about 50m and then we turned left onto a little used track that headed up the side of the mountain. Above on the mountain the mist was slowly drifting away exposing the forest and the point that we were heading for. At first the going was quite easy, but the track petered out and we had to negotiate our way South-south-east through the rough boggy terrain. Cycling became harder and harder as the hill got steeper and to make things even more difficult, we had to weave our way round large boulders that were strewn around the mountain like giant children's building bricks. In places we had to dismount and push the bikes over streams and carry them over rough overgrown patches of prickly gorse. Sweat dripped from us as we toiled up the mountain, even though it was a cold day in January.

After climbing over a steep rise, we came to the old track again, the ground was easier so we mounted our bikes and rode on to the top of the hill. When we reached the fence and the track at the top of the mountain ridge we turned right and cycled through a boggy section until at last we reached the road. At the road the girls were waiting patiently for us, eating crisps and Tracker bars, quite pleased that they had taken the easy way to the top, we just called them wimps! Sometimes you have to lie when you are confronted by women's

Looking towards Carn Ingli

superior logic and this was one of those times. No way were we going to admit that the ride up the side of that mountain had not been the most wonderful and fulfilling experience of a life time. To do so would have been simply letting the side down, and to be honest we had enjoyed it in a crazy masochistic way.

Setting off along the road, we went down the hill for about 50m and then we turned right up a steep grassy bank and came back on to the open mountainside. Heading south-south-west, we rode along a very narrow sheep track that meandered around Foel Eryr. The view down into the valley was wonderful, with the vista of the forests and mountains reflected in the reservoirs of Rosebush and Llys-y-fran. Soon the sheep track started to descend and we just coasted down the mountain, weaving in and out, around boggy and stony stretches. By Pen-lan-wynt farm the path widened out into a track and we descended at ever-increasing speed until we reached the road.

We turned right at the road and then we took a left down a metalled track passing Ty-gwyn Farm. Soon our progress was halted by a metal gate at Penralltddu Farm. We passed through the gate and skirted around the farm buildings until we reached another gate that led into a wet muddy track. Slithering and slipping down the track, we turned right onto an old bridleway that followed a deep valley to our left. In places the bridleway was overgrown and we had to dodge the occasional bramble hanging from the trees. The last part of the track plummeted down into the valley; hanging onto our brakes we avoided the large ruts and stones and careered down to the bottom.

Turning left at the bottom of the track we came to Dan-Coed, a pretty pink house set in the woods. We crossed over a footbridge and came to a gate that led us to the road, this was locked so we had to scramble over the nearby stile and wade across a very muddy stretch. Soon we crossed a bridge over the River Gwaun, and turned right onto the lane that followed the Gwaun Valley back to the picnic site, where we had started our journey earlier in the day. We were very muddy, tired and hungry, but we really had enjoyed our ride around Foel Eryr.

Preseli Mountains – Rides 12, 13, and 14

These rides can be carried out as three separate rides or linked together to make one mega ride covering the whole of the Preseli ridge. You can also link two together and make a mini-mega ride, depending on your fitness.

Instructions for the mega ride.

Start on Ride 14 at the Sychbant picnic site and follow instructions 1 to 7a or 7b. At the track at the top of the mountain you turn left onto the Preseli Ridge track and follow instructions 6 to 7, Ride 13.

Do not turn right onto the cross-road track but go to Ride 12, instruction 3 and follow instructions 3 to 14 (car park at Dan-y-garn).

Join Ride 13 and follow instructions from the car park at Dan-y-garn and follow instructions 9 to 12, and 1 to 5 (Preseli Ridge Track).

At section 5 do not turn right but turn left onto the track and follow Ride 14, instructions 8 to 11.

Instructions for mini-mega ride.

Either join Rides 14 & 13 or Rides 12 & 13 together.

Ride 15: Llys-y-Fran Reservoir and Country Park

Abbreviations: O.R.S. Off-road Section; R.S. Road Section.

Distance: 8 miles.

Time: 2 hours.

Terrain: Forest and open tracks. Easy.

Map: Ordnance Survey Outdoor Leisure Map 35 North Pembrokeshire. No sketch map is included for this ride as the route is easy to follow.

Start and finish: At the car park Llysyfran Reservoir, Grid Reference 040 244.

Before you start this ride, report to the shop as there is a small charge to be paid to complete the circuit. Bikes may also be hired for the hour, half day or day.

The reservoir is set among rolling hills in the north of Pembrokeshire and the undulating perimeter path is an ideal place for off-road cycling. There are a couple of tough climbs at the start. If you want to really have fun, try fording the streams instead of taking the easy way and crossing by the footbridges. Please take extra care when cycling at weekends, especially in the Summer months as the path can get busy. DO NOT SPEED and always GIVE WAY TO WALKERS!

1. Leave the car park and cycle down the hill on the road, with the toilet and shops on your left. Follow the perimeter path in a clockwise direction.

2. Cross the reservoir bridge at the bottom of the dam and climb the steep hill.

3. At the top, ignore the road to your left and continue STRAIGHT on along a track that starts to descend.

4. The directions are quite simple. Just follow the track around the reservoir to the car-park where you started your journey.

You can complete this ride in the opposite direction, but you have to climb the very steep hill at the end of your journey when you are tired.

Llys-y-Fran

The Llys-y-fran dam was built in the late '60s and early '70s to cater for the ever increasing population of Pembrokeshire and the needs of the oil refineries at Milford Haven. This large dam is built across the River Syfynwy, which is a tributary of the Eastern Cleddau.

It is also used as a Country Park and is used for fishing, and dinghy sailing. It is a very pleasant place to spend the day and the surrounding views of the Preseli hills are absolutely beautiful. If you are a keen bird spotter, look out for cormorants, buzzards, sparrowhawks and woodpeckers.

Ride 16: Newcastle Emlyn, Cenarth, Newcastle Emlyn

Abbreviations: O.R.S. Off-road Section; R.S. Road Section.

Distance: 14 miles.

Time: 3 hours.

Terrain: Country lanes and Bridleways, 3 hard climbs. Moderate.

Map: Pathfinder 1011, Newcastle Emlyn.

Start: Cattle Market car park, Newcastle Emlyn. Grid Reference 307 406.

1.   Leave the car park by the toilet block exit and turn LEFT.

2.   Ride into the town and at the T-junction turn RIGHT. Continue to the T-junction at the main A484 road. Turn RIGHT.

3.   Take the second LEFT turning to PENLAN, signposted "To the Swimming Pool." Climb the hill, then take the first turning RIGHT down a small lane, which soon becomes an unsurfaced bridleway.

4.   (O.R.S.) Ride along the bridleway and pass the Vicarage on your right. Go down the hill and cross over the ford. Climb up out of the valley to the T-junction.

5.   (R.S.) At the T-junction turn LEFT. Climb the steep hill passing Penwaun Farm on your right and carry on to the cross-roads. This is a really long climb.

6.   At the cross-roads by the telephone box turn RIGHT and go down towards Cenarth. Ride on to the main A484 road.

7.   Turn LEFT, and follow the main road into Cenarth. It is well worth stopping here and looking at the waterfalls and the Old Watermill. Just before the bridge on the right is the Cenarth Tea Room where they serve food all day, and they make a good cup of tea.

8. After looking around the village, cross over the bridge and carry on along the A484 for a short distance to the first turning on your right which goes up another steep hill.

9. Turn RIGHT and climb the hill. Ignore the left turning to Pen y Graig Farm, on your right the hillside plunges down through the trees to the river in the valley. Go round a left-hand bend and go down the hill. At the bottom of the hill the road goes round a right-hand bend; carry STRAIGHT on to a road marked as a RUP on the map, passing a white house on your right.

10. (O.R.S.) Ride on the RUP to a farm on your right. Go STRAIGHT on through an iron farm gate into an old green lane; climb up the slight hill to another iron gate. Pass through this gate and head across the open field, bearing left to another gate. Pass through this gate and head straight on for the next gate ahead of you, which takes you into another green lane. Ride along the old lane to a T-junction where you turn RIGHT.

11. (R. S.) Climb up the steep hill to the T-junction at the B4570 where you turn LEFT. On your left is a wonderful view of the Preseli Mountains stretching out across the horizon.

12. Ride on the B4570 and take your first RIGHT, after about 200m. Take the first turning on your RIGHT and go down into the valley. After crossing the bridge, you come to a T-junction at Porth-y-fynwent. This farm must be a free zoo for they have every type of farm animal on show.

13. Turn LEFT and climb out of the valley. This is the worst hill on the journey, so take your time. Pass the old church of St Mary's at Brongwyn on your left and ride STRAIGHT on at the cross-roads (the road to the left at this cross-roads is a No Through Road). Carry on to another cross-roads.

14. Go STRAIGHT on at the cross-roads and continue down the hill ignoring the roads to your right and your left. Soon after the road goes round a right-hand bend you will see a turning to your right by Cwnsilltyn Farm.

15. Turn RIGHT and go down the steep hill through the woods.

Ignore the fork to your left and the track off to your left. Cross over the river bridge and at Cwmdu Cottage, on your left, the road goes round a right-hand bend and starts a sharp climb. Just as you think you have climbed enough, to your right you will see a bridleway going down into the wood.

16. (O.R.S) Turn RIGHT onto the bridleway and plunge down the hill. At the fork in the tracks keep RIGHT and ride on to the road and cottages at Pont-Ceri.

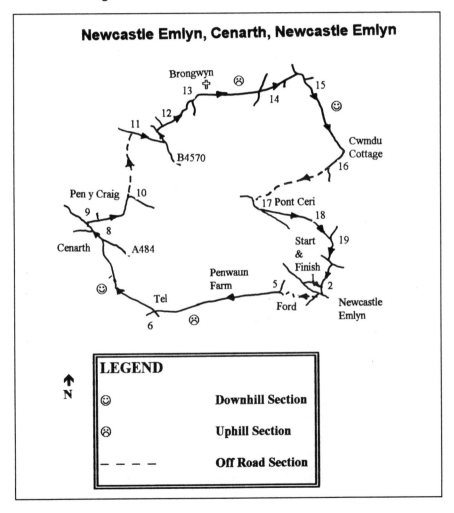

Newcastle Emlyn, Cenarth, Newcastle Emlyn

LEGEND

☺ Downhill Section

☹ Uphill Section

– – – – Off Road Section

17. (R.S.) Turn LEFT onto the road with a stone wall on the right (ahead of you is the B4333, which you ignore).

18. Climb the hill, which has a great view out over the river valley and Newcastle Emlyn on your right. You reach a T-junction with an old post box set in a house wall to your right.

19. Turn RIGHT at the T-junction and go down hill into Newcastle Emlyn.

20. At the bottom of the hill, ignore the roads to your right and left and cross over the old river bridge. Ride up the main street of Newcastle Emlyn with its pubs, craft and antique shops, to the car parking sign on your right.

21. Turn RIGHT and you are soon back at the Mart car park where you started your journey.

Cenarth

Cenarth is a picturesque village on the River Teifi, which is famous for its waterfall and salmon, which can be seen leaping up the river. Next to the falls is the old flour mill with a unique collection of

The Old Mill, Cenarth Falls

coracles from around the world, and you can see how they are made and used. It is however only open from Easter until the end of October. It is now a conservation village and many of its old buildings have been restored. The Old Smithy contains a very interesting exhibition of original smithy equipment and many Victorian exhibits, and what's more entry to the exhibition is free! The 'Alehouse by the Church' is the oldest building in the village dating back to medieval times, and is built on the original site of the old ale house belonging to the Monastic community of St Llawddog.

Newcastle Emlyn

The riverside town of Newcastle Emlyn is like a journey back in time. It is a typical example of an old Welsh farming town. The shops all have a strange quaintness of their own, very different to shopping in the city!

The town derives its name from the 'New Castle' which was built around 1240 by Maredudd ap Rhys to defend the town. There is not much left surviving as it didn't survive the Roundhead fire when Newcastle Emlyn was garrisoned for the king during the Civil War.

How was it for us?

It was a warm afternoon in July when we left the car park in the sleepy farming town of Newcastle Emlyn. The plan was to cycle to Cenarth falls and stop for lunch before continuing our ride.

We turned left out of the Mart car park, and rode for a short distance before turning right at the T-junction. We continued through the town until we reached the next T-junction and turned right onto the main road. When we reached the second road on the left, which was signposted to the Swimming pool, we turned left, and rapidly changed down our gears when we saw the hill looming ahead. Halfway up this pretty, but steep, hill was a turning to our right which looked like a small road. We turned into this and within a short time it changed into a narrow track.

After cycling past the vicarage on our right we descended a hill and came to a ford. Dave couldn't resist madly cycling through this, but remembering a recent ducking in a river I decided to err on the side of caution and cross over on the bridge. We continued uphill out of the valley and turned left at the T-junction.

I let out a long groan. Ahead of us was a really long steep hill. Dave, otherwise known as "We're nearly at the top" bounded on ahead as I slowly struggled up, my heart pounding and my legs turning to jelly. At last, we reached the top and some cross-roads. There was an old fashioned red telephone box on the corner where we turned right, this was something I had not seen for a long time.

The road descended steeply: this was the type of riding I liked! We tore down the hill watching our cycle computers at last go into double figures. The road passed through some trees and strangely in the hot afternoon it felt as if it was raining. It must have been the moisture from the trees dropping onto my sweating body, but anyway, it felt good. Soon we reached the main road into Cenarth. Cenarth is an extremely attractive village, famous for the beautiful Cenarth Falls. These are quite small in the summer, but if you go there in the winter they are like a wild boiling cauldron. There is a lovely walk alongside the river – an idea for another day! It is worth going to have a look at the Old Watermill on the side of the river, and also the Coracle Museum. Coracles have been the traditional method of transport up and down the river for the local fishermen for many decades, and it is quite fascinating to see how they are made. There are also several very good craft shops in this village if you want to look around and buy some souvenirs.

We arrived in Cenarth at exactly 2.33pm, and parked our bikes outside the pub. We hungrily examined the menu, and hastened inside to order. Imagine our disappointment when we were told, "Sorry, we stopped serving food at 2.30." This may not be so bad when travelling by car, but it is a real downer after you have cycled there! However, all was not lost. Next door to the pub was the excellent Cenarth Falls Tea Rooms, and here we managed to get a very welcome ham salad and a cup of tea. Round the back there is a model village.

Suitably refreshed we left Cenarth, and crossed over the river bridge. The day was getting cooler and there was a definite nip in the air, which was just as well, because within a few metres we turned right up yet another steep hill. There is a museum on the left but today we did not stop as we needed to get home before tea time. We slogged up the hill and within a short distance we were sweating profusely, even though we had entered a wooded section that plummeted on our right, down to the river 100m below. Thankfully at the top of the hill the road descended into a valley so here was a chance to get our breath back and free-wheel to the bottom. All too soon on the valley floor we forked left and headed along a bridleway, passed through an iron field gate and rode past an old farm on our right. Within 100m we came to another field gate which we opened with difficulty and rode across three open fields, towards a way-mark post that we could see in the distance. We entered an old green lane that must have been used for hundreds of years, the hedges on both sides hanging with the weight of juicy blackberries. We had a drink, ate a few blackberries, and cycled on until we came to a road.

Dave had told me it was going to be an easy ride today, but before me was yet another steep hill which seemed to go on, and on. Around every bend the road seemed to climb at an alarming rate. When we reached the B4570 road we turned left and at last the road levelled out; there on our left was an incredible view of the Preseli Mountains. This was our excuse for a stop, not that we really needed one! It was here that an elderly woman from a house to our right asked us "Are you all right dears?" We explained that we had stopped to look at the view, and she was delighted when we said how lucky she was to live in such a wonderful place.

In 200m we turned right and right again. This was bliss; the road at last started to descend, so I held my breath, let go the brakes and raced after Dave to the bottom of the valley. We crossed over a small bridge and at a T-junction where we turned left, there was the strangest farm I have ever seen. There must have been every conceivable farm animal in and around the small outbuildings, pigs, goats, horses, sheep, chickens, an assortment of cats of every colour and four barking dogs. To see such a profusion of animals in such a small place is unusual, to say the least.

After we passed the farm the road narrowed and to my astonishment started to climb in the most alarming fashion. This was the worst hill of the ride, there were no bends just a straight road to the top of what looked like a small mountain. The steepness soon defeated me; Dave plodded on, but even he had to give up way before the top. Halfway up the hill we came to the lovely old church of St Mary's at Brongwyn; the Medieval building was set behind a secluded screen of old yew trees. We paused for a time; looked around the churchyard and made one more effort to push on to the top of the hill.

We went straight over the cross-roads at the top of the hill and the road, at last, began to descend. It was with great delight that we raced towards the valley floor. By Cwnsilltyn Farm we took a sharp right fork and it was here that a young cyclist sped past us at an alarming rate. At the bottom of the hill the young man was waiting to speak to us. He introduced himself as Jake, and went on to tell us that this route was his regular training ride. So the three of us rode on over a bridge, passed by Cwmdu Cottage and climbed a short hill until we reached a bridleway to our right. Jake told us that the next section was great because it ran downhill alongside the river to Pont-Ceri and that it was his favourite path. Soon the path plummeted downwards and Jake sped off with Dave trying to keep up with him. Within 100m Jake and Dave had disappeared into the woods. Later at the bottom of the hill Dave was waiting for me, of Jake there was no sign. Within a mile of riding through the trees we came across Jake again, and we rode along chatting until we reached the road at Pont-Ceri, we shook hands and parted, Jake turned right and we turned left.

This was the last section of the ride. We climbed a hill and turned right by an old post box and then headed down the hill into Newcastle Emlyn. We crossed over the old river bridge and cycled up the main street with its quaint little shops and pubs. Nearly at the end of the main street we turned right and within 100m we were back at the Mart car park where we had started our journey. It had been a very enjoyable but exhausting day.

Brechfa Forest: the Region

Brechfa Forest is one of the best-kept secrets of south-west Wales. This beautiful region of mountains and forest just north of Carmarthen is still unspoilt and almost deserted. Although we have lived in this area for nearly thirty years, Brechfa was still unknown to us until a young man in a bike shop in Carmarthen told us about the wonderful off-road trails that criss-cross this area. We have ridden the three rides at different times of the year and have never seen more than four people on our journeys.

The forest is owned and maintained by Forest Enterprise Wales which is part of the Forestry Commission, and they have been extremely helpful to us in the preparation of these rides. Occasionally trails may have to be closed for your safety when work is being carried out, so please heed the signs. These trails are often used by horse riders, so please be considerate to them as they may be startled by your bike. There is plenty of room in these forests for all.

A wonderful time to go riding in the Brechfa Forest, if you like a challenge, is in the Winter when the snow is on the ground. You could almost imagine yourself in the middle of a Christmas card, with the fir trees all delicately tipped with snow. In the summertime it's a different place again, with the sun blazing down through the trees. It's a truly wonderful area; nowhere is the woodland too dense and because of this there is an abundance of wild life and wild flowers.

Don't forget to take your picnic when going to the Brechfa Forest. There are plenty of picnic sites throughout the forest in really delightful locations, and the picnic site at Abergorlech even has a barbecue for you to use – supply your own coals though!

Ride 17: Brechfa Forest from Brechfa Picnic Site

Abbreviations: O.R.S. Off-road Section; R.S. Road Section.

Distance: 12 miles.

Time: 3 hours.

Terrain: Good forest tracks and short stretch of country lane. 2 long climbs. Hard.

Map: Pathfinder 1035 Pencader or Landranger 146 Lampeter, Llandovery.

Start and finish: At the picnic site, Grid Reference 522 322, 2 miles north of Brechfa village. Brechfa is roughly 9 miles north of Carmarthen town. There is limited parking at the picnic site.

In Brechfa Forest

The Ride

1. (R.S.) Leave the picnic site and turn LEFT onto the road and go
down the hill.

2. (O.R.S.) In a quarter of a mile you will come to a sharp right-hand
bend. To your RIGHT you will see a wooden gate into the forest
at grid reference 523 319, go through this gate and go down on
this track until you come to a river bridge.

3. Cross over the river bridge and at the T-junction of tracks turn
RIGHT. Follow this track, ignoring the small track off to your left,
keeping the River Marlais down in the valley to your right. The
track starts a long gradual climb to a fork in the tracks.

4. At the fork in the tracks, take the smaller track to your RIGHT up
a steep hill, with the open moorland of Myndd Llafihangel-rhos-
y-corn to your right. After you have climbed this hill you won't
have the breath to say this mouthful. Keep climbing to a gate
near to the road at Crug-y-Beow, grid reference 498 355.

5. Go through the gate and turn LEFT on to the road towards the
radio mast. After 200m turn LEFT again, go through another gate
and follow this track back into the forest.

6. Keep STRAIGHT on the main track ignoring 2 cross-roads that
have lesser tracks to your left and right to a fork in the tracks.

7. At the fork in the tracks, with a track coming up the hill from your
left turn RIGHT, and in about 200m at the cross-roads of tracks
turn LEFT.

8. Go down the hill to the next cross-roads. Here go STRAIGHT
on, and go up a small hill for a short distance and turn LEFT at
the T-junction. This is a strange junction – more like a large traffic
island; we all went in different directions but we all arrived at the
T-junction at the same time.

9. Cycle on to a cross-roads of tracks where you turn LEFT. This
track is marked on the ordnance survey map as a bridleway and
a footpath.

10. Keep to this track to a cross-roads of tracks, where you go

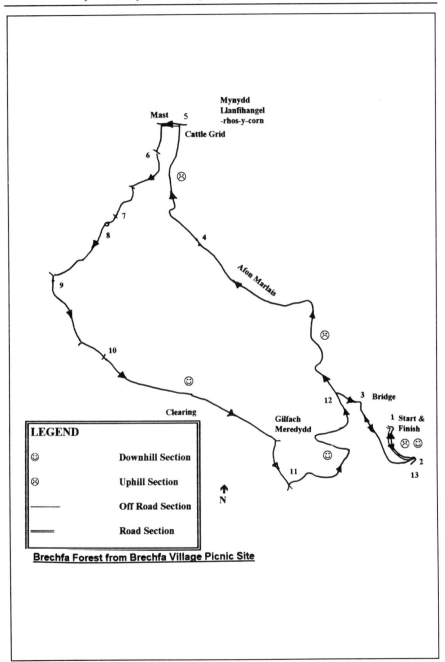

Brechfa Forest from Brechfa Village Picnic Site

STRAIGHT on at grid reference 490 330. Continue on the main track, ignoring the tracks to your left and your right. Go past a clearing to your right and ride on to a field gate.

11. Go through the gate onto a metalled track, ignore the track to your left to Gilfach Meredydd, and at the cross-roads turn LEFT onto an unsurfaced track at grid reference 509 317. Tie your hats on for the downhill section, and what a descent. Please take care on the bends.

12. At the bridge at the bottom of hill turn RIGHT; you crossed this bridge earlier at the beginning of your ride.

13. Climb up the hill to the gate, go through the gate and turn LEFT onto the road.

14. (R.S.) Climb up the road for a ¼ of a mile and turn RIGHT into a picnic site where you started and finish your ride.

Ride 18: Brechfa Forest from Abergorlech Picnic Site

Abbreviations: O.R.S. Off-road Section; R.S. Road Section.

Distance: 10 miles.

Time: 3 hours.

Terrain: Good forest tracks, one long climb, Moderate.

Map: Pathfinder 1035 Pencader or Landranger 146 Lampeter, Llandovery.

Start and finish: At the picnic site, grid reference 586 337 in Abergorlech.

---

1. Leave the picnic site through the gate into the forest at the north end of the car park.

2. Follow the track with the River Gorlech on your left and ignore the track to your right. The track here is way marked with white and red marks.

3. Take the second track on your LEFT and cross over the river bridge; the track starts a long winding climb up a hill. After a while you will come to a gate blocked with a pile of boulders, pass this on your left and proceed onwards up the hill.

4. When you reach the top of the hill go STRAIGHT on over the cross-roads. The track is way-marked with red signs.

5. Go down the hill and fork RIGHT.

6. Within a few hundred metres, go STRAIGHT on at the slightly staggered cross-roads named Rhandir-gini on the Pathfinder map, towards Allt Esgair-onen-fawr.

7. Take the next RIGHT turn onto a track at grid reference 564 339.

8. This track circles around the mountain with the River Nany y Ffin and Banc Farm to your left, way down in the valley. Ignore the

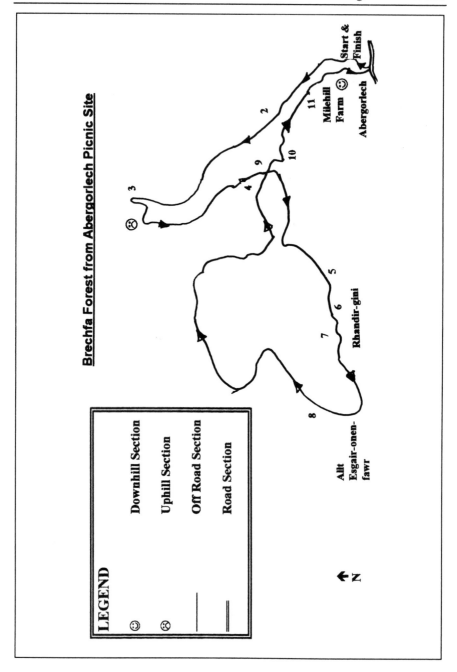

Brechfa Forest from Abergorlech Picnic Site

Start & Finish

Milehill Farm

Abergorlech

Rhandir-gini

Allt Esgair-onen-fawr

LEGEND

☺ Downhill Section

☹ Uphill Section

Off Road Section

Road Section

N

two tracks to your left and the five tracks to your right. You will see red waymarks on your way.

9. At the cross-roads, go STRAIGHT on down the hill. This is the cross-roads you crossed earlier.

10. When you reach a T-junction of tracks turn LEFT and follow the red waymarks. The track becomes much narrower and rocky. Watch your speed here because two of our party parted with their bikes on this stretch.

11. Go down the old lane, passing the turning to Milehill Farm on your right, to the road and Abergorlech. At the road turn LEFT and cross over the river bridge, then turn LEFT into the picnic site where you started. If you feel like a drink and a rest turn right at the road and visit the Red Lion pub 50m on your right.

Barbara admiring the view in Brechfa Forest

Ride 19: Brechfa Forest from Rhydcymerau

Abbreviations: O.R.S. Off-road Section; R.S. Road Section.

Distance: 15 miles.

Time: 4 hours.

Terrain: Good Forest tracks and one stretch of road; two climbs; moderate.

Map: Pathfinder 1035 Pencader.

Start and finish: At picnic site, Grid Reference 588 377 south of Rhydcymerau off the B4337.

---

1. Start at the picnic site and leave at the entrance. Turn LEFT onto the B4337 and ride on to Rhydcymerau. Pass the pub on your right (not open in the day time) and carry on to the fork in the roads.

2. Fork LEFT and ride out of the village for about 200m to a cross-roads of tracks, marked as a bridleway on the map.

3. Turn LEFT and climb the hill. The track soon becomes rough and wet but carry on, go through a gate and pass Pwllclymbyd Cottage on your left. Go down the hill and go around the left-hand bend. You reach a cross-roads of tracks at Trawscoed Uchaf House.

4. When you reach the cross-roads go STRAIGHT on, climb the slight hill until you soon reach a track T-junction, where you turn RIGHT.

5. You are now in the valley of the River Gorlech. Follow this track with the river on your right ignoring all tracks to your right and your left to a wooden gate. Pass through this gate and you are at the picnic site at Abergorlech. You can do two things, have a

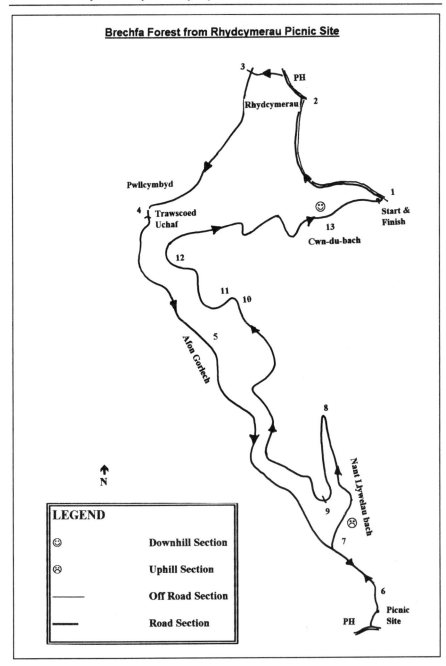

Brechfa Forest from Rhydcymerau Picnic Site

picnic here or carry on to the road turn right and ride on for about 200m to the Public House on your right, for a welcome drink.

6. After your picnic or drink return to the gate at the picnic site. Pass through and retrace your ride up the hill to the first track on your right, marked with a white waymark.

7. Turn RIGHT here and start the long climb with the Nant Llywelau bach (brook) on your right. Ignore the tracks to your left and your right. When you are almost at the top of the climb you come to a sharp left-hand bend with a track going off to your right, again way marked with a white post

8. Turn LEFT and continue to a track cross-roads.

9. At the cross-roads go STRAIGHT on, ignore the track to your right and cycle on to a fork in the tracks.

10. When you reach the fork take the RIGHT fork and climb the hill. When you reach the top of the hill you go around a left-hand bend and enter a clearing at a track cross-roads. Grid reference 573 368.

11. Go STRAIGHT on at the cross-roads and you soon start to descend. Ignore the tracks to your left and your right.

12. Keep on this main track as it bends around the top of the mountain with the river far below you on your left. Ignore all the tracks off to your right and your left, and ride on down the steep descent towards Cwmdubach Farm to a track T-junction.

13. At the T-junction turn RIGHT and go down to the picnic site on your LEFT where you started your journey.

How was it for us?

The Brechfa Forest in West Wales is a wonderful area of mountainous forest just north of Carmarthen which seems to be completely neglected by tourists who flock to the coast during the summer months. Considering that they drive so close to this area along the A40 you would have thought that somebody would have realised that it was well worth a visit. The terrain is mixed woodland criss-crossed with tracks that lead down into sheltered valleys where small villages untouched by time, nestle by bubbling rivers. Once in these villages you can sit in the local Inn, sink a pint, sing songs with the locals and discuss the virtues of Welsh and English rugby – for this area is Welsh through and through.

Barbara and I set out to complete this ride on a hot day in July. We arrived at the Rhydcymerau picnic site at about 10am and we decided to turn left out of the picnic site and ride along the road towards Rhydcymerau. As we rode along through the wooded valley a morning mist still hung over the river on our left, and sunbeams shafting through the trees seemed to dance across the road to some silent tune. A heron disturbed from his breakfast by our chatting, soared up from the river and crossed the road in full flight to disappear over the trees. This easy road section seemed to go as we had planned, it warmed our muscles and prepared us for the harder off-road sections that lay ahead.

Rhydcymerau is only small and within seconds we had passed through it and we were heading down a narrow lane towards our next turning. Within 200m we turned left onto a rough bridleway and started to climb up a short steep hill. The track became rocky and muddy and we had to weave in and out of the large puddles while we dodged the rocks. At the top of the hill we came to an iron field gate which we passed through and then we descended a hill, passing Pwllclymbyd Cottage on our left. An elderly lady was out working in the garden; she seemed surprised to see somebody cycling on this little used bridleway. We exchanged pleasantries and carried on with our journey. A little further on we passed Trawscoed Uchaf House and at a cross-roads of tracks we went straight on and turned right into the valley of the River Gorlech.

The morning was quite warm and here in the valley it was simply marvellous. To our right the River Gorlech meandered along the valley floor through forested hills of various greens. The track was wide and had a good surface so we just rode along enjoying the beautiful scenery, stopping every so often to look at birds and wild flowers that we passed. For an hour we slowly rode along this picturesque valley until we met a lady who was fastening signs to a tree. She told us that in two days time that there was to be a horse trial through the forest and it was her job to erect the markers for the riders to follow. We talked for a time, then said our good-byes and cycled onwards. After a short climb we reached a gate at Abergorlech picnic site, we passed through the gate and we decided to ride down to the village and stop at the Black Lion Inn.

Abergorlech is a pretty village with whitewashed cottages, a tiny shop and one of the best inns in West Wales. We sat in the garden overlooking the river, ate crisps washed down with a bitter shandy and chatted to a group of locals; this was sheer bliss on a wonderful summer's day. Relaxed and rested we climbed back onto our bikes and started to retrace our path back into the woods. Just as we were about to leave the village I noticed that my back tyre was as flat as a pancake. A gentleman in the nearby cottage noticing my plight came out and asked me if I would like to come into his garden to mend the puncture. I thanked him for his kind offer but told him that I would just replace the tube with a spare one. I wonder if you would get the same offer of help in London or Birmingham.

When we entered the woods we followed the white way marks and turned right on a track that climbed alongside Nant Llywelau brook. This was the first really hard climb on the journey and it was a stinker! The hill slowly wound its way up the side of the mountain until we reached a steep hairpin bend where our legs finally gave up the ghost and we had to push our bikes over the brow of the hill. Gasping for breath at the top we leapt back on and soared down the track to be able to climb over the next rise. Piles of logs stood beside the track looking like telegraph poles without a home. The river Gorlech looked small and insignificant, down in the valley. We were climbing slowly upwards around the side of the mountain ignoring all the tracks off to our left and right. At last, the main track finally climbed 100m and levelled out; to our left at the bottom of the mountain we could see Trawscoed Uchaf House looking like a small doll's house beside the river.

The forest track curved down the side of the mountain, we held on tight and set off. It was like being on a gigantic switchback as we sped down the mountain. Trees flashed past on both sides of the track and the bends came at you, first to the right and then to the left. Suddenly we hit a wet section at speed and the spray was thrown into the air, creating miniature rainbows. Finally at the bottom of the hill we turned right at a track T-junction and descended down to the picnic site where we had started our ride. We had excellent weather and we had really enjoyed our journey, so we made a promise to return to Brechfa Forest.

Dave struggling uphill in Brechfa Forest

Appendices

Sales & Repair

Bierspool Cycles, London Road, Pembroke Dock. Tel: 01646 68103.

Enterprise Cycles, Unit 52, Honeyborough Industrial Estate, Neyland. Tel: 01646 601014.

Mikes Bikes, 17 Prendergast, Haverfordwest. Tel: 01437 760068.

Ar Dy Feic, 20b King Street, Carmarthen. Tel: 01267 221182

M&P Cycles, Unit 4/5 Castell Close, Llamsamlet, Swansea. Tel: 01792 700396.

Wheelies, 34 Uplands Crescent, Uplands, Swansea. Tel: 01792 472612.

Bike Hire

Ar Dy Feic, 20b King Street, Carmarthen. Tel: 01267 221182.

Bro Bikes, 3 Ashley House, Frog Street, Tenby. Tel: 01834 844766

Haven Sports, Marine Rd, Broadhaven. Tel: 01437 781354

LLysmebbyg Guest House, East St Newport, Pembrokeshire. Tel 01239 820008

Llysyfran Reservoir & Country Park, Clarbeston Rd. Tel: 01437 532 273/694 (For riding round the dam only)

Mikes Bikes, 17 Prendergast, Haverfordwest. Tel: 01437 760068.

Preseli Venture, Parcynole Fach, Mathry. Tel: 01348 837709

Roch Cycle hire, Mark & Julie's Supermarket, Roch. Tel: 01437 710280 or 71637.

Tenby Cycle Hire, Sergeants Lane, St Julian Street, Tenby. Tel: 01834 845955.

The Post Office Stores, Abergorlech. Tel: 01558 685211.

Tourist Information Centres

Tenby, The Croft. Tel: 01834 842402

Pembroke, The Common. Tel: 01646 622388

Haverfordwest, The Old Bridge. Tel: 01437 763110

Fishguard, Hamilton Terrace. Tel: 01348 873484

Cardigan, Theatr Mwldan. Tel: 01239 613230

Carmarthen, Lammas St. Tel: 01267 231557

Other titles of interest from:

WALKS IN MYSTERIOUS WALES

Laurence Main

Follow the spirit paths of Wales - visit the most sacred and secret sites and discover ancient traditions of this historic country in the company of a leading expert. And, while you're discovering Welsh heritage, enjoy some excellent walks across the length and breadth of the country.

(£7.95)

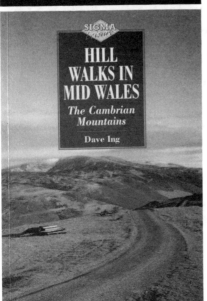

HILL WALKS IN MID WALES
The Cambrian Mountains

Dave Ing

This is one of the very few books to explore the pleasures of walking in Mid Wales - far from from the big mountains of Snowdonia and away from the crowds, yet so accessible for a day in the hills.

(£7.95)

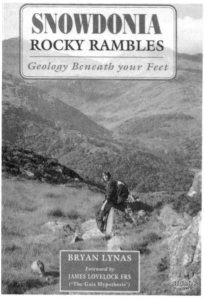

SNOWDONIA ROCKY RAMBLES: Geology Beneath Your Feet

Bryan Lynas

This, the companion volume to *Lakeland Rocky Rambles*, is much more than a book of mountain walks. Each of the ten walks is a voyage of discovery and a journey through time, with insights into the geology, wildlife and history of these splendid peaks. With a foreword by James Lovelock FRS.

(£9.95)

BEST PUB WALKS IN SNOWDONIA

Laurence Main

Whether your fancy is a strenuous hike up Snowdon or a leisurely amble in the foothills, there's the perfect pub walk for you in this book. There's a huge variety here - with the assurance of a welcome for weary walkers in all the pubs en route. Take in coastal and estuary views, lakes, waterfalls, forests, castles, standing stones and steam trains, all topped off with the local liquid refreshment!

(£6.95)

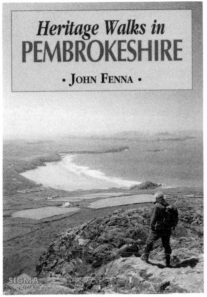

HERITAGE WALKS IN PEMBROKESHIRE

John Fenna

Pembrokeshire contains not just stunning beaches and cliff scenery, it hold a wealth of historical and prehistoric remains. Enjoy this selection of circular walks whilst learning about the rich heritage - natural, historic and legendary - of Pembrokeshire.

£6.95

WALKING THE BRECON BEACONS AND THE BLACK MOUNTAINS

David Hunter

This is a collection of 30 circular walks in the Brecon Beacons National Park, ranging from 3 to 13 miles in length. It introduces walkers to a countryside of many moods and gives local background information. Excellent photographs and exquisite sketch maps add visual interest to the accurate route descriptions.

(£7.95)

CYCLING IN NORTH WALES

Philip Routledge

North Wales offers dramatic scenery and this book will take you through the best of it. There are many challenging hills and Philip adds a point of special interest to each ride - be it rare flora or fauna, or a fascinating cultural insight.

(£6.95)

CYCLING IN SOUTH WALES

Rosemary Evans

Containing a wide collection of routes for both families and energetic riders, this cycling book takes you from the River Severn to the Irish Sea! The routes can be connected by long distance cycle tourers, or taken in isolation for a good day out for the less serious biker.

(£7.95)